ASSASSIN!

THE DEADLY ART OF THE CULT OF THE ASSASSINS

ASSASSIN!

THE DEADLY ART OF THE CULT OF THE ASSASSINS

Dr. Haha Lung

CITADEL PRESS

Kensington Publishing Corp.

www.kensingtonbooks.com

Also by Dr. Haha Lung

The Ancient Art of Assassination
The Black Science: Ancient and Modern Techniques of Ninja Mind
   Manipulation (with Christopher B. Prowant)
Knights of Darkness: Secrets of the World's Deadliest Night Fighters
Shadowhand: The History and Secrets of Ninja Taisavaki
   (with Christopher B. Prowant)

CITADEL PRESS BOOKS are published by

Kensington Publishing Corp.
850 Third Avenue
New York, NY 10022

Previously published by Paladin Press

All Kensington titles, imprints, and distributed lines are available at special
quantity discounts for bulk purchases for sales promotions, premiums,
fund-raising, educational, or institutional use. Special book excerpts or
customized printings can also be created to fit specific needs. For details,
write or phone the office of the Kensington special sales manager:
Kensington Publishing Corp., 850 Third Avenue, New York, NY 10022,
attn: Special Sales Department, phone 1-800-221-2647.

First printing: October 2004

10   9   8   7   6   5   4   3   2

Printed in the United States of America

Cataloging data may be obtained from the Library of Congress

ISBN 0-8065-2620-3

Contents

DISCLAIMER

Opinions expressed in this book are those of the author. At no time does this book advocate the use of violence against the *peaceful* practitioners of any religion. This book is for use as a historical reference and for understanding *defensive* techniques against attackers. The author, publisher, and distributors of this book are not responsible for the use or misuse of any information or techniques described in this book, and penalties for the illegal use or misuse of any of the information or techniques discussed herein may be punishable under the law. *This book is for academic study only.*

A NOTE ON SPELLING

This text contains many words translated from Arabic. To insure that the reader is not burdened by different translations of the same word (Mohammad and Mohamet, Koran and Quran, Muslim and Moslem), a glossary appears at the end of the book.

The term "Assassin" in this book is uppercased because it is used as a proper noun, i.e., "The Assassin [a member of the Order of Assassins] killed the emir with a poisoned dagger." Unless the term is used to refer to a killer who was or is not linked to the Order of Assassins, it is uppercased.

The term "Templars," i.e., Knights Templars, appears plural, but this is not the case. The term has an unusual spelling that makes it appear plural. Even a single member of this organization is correctly called a Templars.

Timeline

So that the reader is not overwhelmed with dates, places, and events, I have encapsulated the critical events in the history revolving around the Order of Assassins. Starting 3,000 years before Christ appeared and running all the way to 1492, I point out the events you should be familiar with, but I also overlap this timeline by 400 years with more detailed text so that you see in detail what happened between Hasan ibn Sabbah's appearance on the scene in the 11th century and the Muslim's ejection from the Iberian Peninsula.

• • • • •

3000 b.c.e.
Great Flood destroys Ka'Ba.

570 c.e.
Mohammed the prophet born in Mecca.

605 c.e.
Ka'Ba shrine rebuilt.

622 c.e.
Mohammed flees Mecca for Medina; Islamic era begins.

632 c.e.

Mohammed dies; Abu Bakr appointed first Caliph.

634 c.e.

Abu Bakr dies; Omar appointed second Caliph.

644 c.e.

Omar murdered by Persian slave; Othmann appointed third Caliph. Shiite sect recognized with Ali as leader; Shiites challenge Othmann.

656 c.e.

Othmann murdered; Ali declared Caliph.

657 c.e.

Shiites and Sunnis clash at Siffin.

661 c.e.

Ali murdered in mosque at Karabala; Muawiya declared Caliph; Umayyad Dynasty begins; Ali's first son (Hassan) dies, believed poisoned by Muawiya supporters.

680 c.e.

Hussain, Ali's second son, slain by governor of Kufa's forces; Hussain's head sent to Yazid.

732 c.e.

Muslims defeated by French army under Karl Martel at Battle of Tours.

750 c.e.

Abbasid Dynasty succeeds Umayyad Dynasty.

969 c.e.

Ismaili Shiites conquer Egypt and establish Fatimid Dynasty.

1004 c.e.

Dar-ul-Hikmat ("Grand Lodge") established in Cairo.

1070 c.e.
   Hasan ibn Sabbah born in Persia.

1090 c.e.
   Hasan prepared for battle with Order of Assassins.

1092 c.e.
   Grand Vizier Nizam al-Mulk assassinated with a poisoned knife blade by a "holy man" in Turkey.

1095 c.e.
   Crusades begin.

1123 c.e.
   Grand Lodge destroyed by invading Turks.

1171 c.e.
   Saladin conquers Fatimid Dynasty.

1260 c.e.
   Rukn ad-Din Baibars leads revolt of Mamelukes; Mameluke Dynasty begins.

1492 c.e.
   Muslims ejected from Iberian Peninsula.

Acknowledgments

Thanks to Peter Gilbert, Lenox Cramer, Frank "Black Mantis" Brown, and the Warriors of the Zendokan: James L. Shifferly, Melvin Zickefoose Jr., and Marcus Woods.

Special thanks to Sufi Abdullah Hakiem Zarief (aka Roger Coleman) and to "B.N.", the little Muslim afraid for his name to appear here.

Introduction

"The Kingdom of the Father is like a man who wants to kill an important person. In his house he unsheathed the sword and stuck it in the wall to assure himself that his hand would be firm. Then he killed the person."

—The Gnostic Gospel of Thomas

THE MYTH OF THE ASSASSIN

Ours is not the first generation in the West to live in fear of fanatical killers spilling out of the Middle East, blood in their eye, poison on their blades. Since the Middle Ages, many a killer has deservedly earned the appellation *assassin*. But who were the first? What was this terrorist cult of accomplished killers that cut a wide and bloody gash across the face of the Middle East before stabbing at the very heart of Europe?

They were the dreaded Cult of Hashishins, a cadre of accomplished slayers so feared that their name became a Western synonym for cold-blooded killers: Assassin!

Down through the ages this cult of shadowy killers has been seen as a group of true believers by some, mercenary killers hiding behind the convenient cloak of religion by most. Today, much about them is still shrouded in mystery, wrapped in dispute, and cloaked in controversy and confusion. Even the origin of the name itself is contested.

We are told the first Western use of the word *assassin* appears in Dante's *Inferno*—"Lo perfido assassin"—and implies a killer for

1

hire. Yet long before Dante took quill in hand, the existence of a secretive brotherhood of ruthless killers—shape-shifting half-man, half-jinn demons that no latch could lock out, no bodyguard protect against—was whispered about at many an oasis, in mosques, and behind barred doors from Cairo to Istanbul. Yes, Middle Eastern kings and princes had long known what European princes and knights adventuring into the Holy Land would soon come to know and fear. Waking to find a dagger buried in their pillow, Middle Eastern potentates, diplomats, and generals were quick to recognize the unsoiled blade for the clear message it was: A friendly request from the "Old Man of the Mountain"—master Assassin Hasan ibn Sabbah—to curb an unpopular policy; an invitation to quietly resign from office; an order to break off a pogrom against a particular tribe or village favored by the Assassin grand master. Soon enough, the armored invaders from Europe would learn.

Fearless when facing sunlit scimitars on bright battlefields of glory, ready to lay down their lives at a moment's notice for lord and crown, even the bravest of European knights quickly learned to quake at the thought of an Assassin's poisoned cup that no man could guard against; the silent strangler's cord dropped by an Assassin from above, and the unseen Assassin's dirk striking from the shadows.

You can't fight what you can't see.

This was the lesson European crusaders learned the hard way, which is the same lesson those of us in the West today are having to relearn in the face of Middle Eastern terrorism.

But today we have advantages those first crusaders didn't. First, we know the beast's name: Assassin! We know how he prefers striking from the shadows, from behind, when and where least expected. Second, we can unearth his history, his past motivations, methods, and murders in order to better predict his future attacks. Finally, we can study and master his manipulative tricks and killing techniques to, when necessary, fight fire with fire by turning his techniques of terror against him.

By studying these first of the genuine Assassins—those credited with inventing myriad techniques of terror still in use today—we can more easily protect ourselves and our loved ones against today's assassins.

What moved and motivated this cadre of killers? Were they truly religious fanatics fed on the promise that death in battle meant immediate transmission to Heaven? Or was wealth and earthly power their only motivation? How was it that their influence spread both East and West, spawning deadly secret societies in Europe, influencing Far Eastern killer-cadres such as the dreaded Thuggee stranglers of India and the ninja killers of Japan? Is it true these dark-cloaked medieval Assassins originated (or at least refined to high art) techniques of terror and slaughter still practiced today by dozens of killer cults and cadres, many of whom take pride in tracing their lethal lineage back to these medieval killers?

We know without a doubt the myth of the Assassins spread to Europe and beyond. What about their murderous madness? It is said they are responsible for importing miraculous cures and the deadliest of poisons into Europe. Is this truth or mere metaphor? Is it true they worshipped the severed head of a long-forgotten pre-Islamic god, and did they spread his killer cult to Europe? Is it true they seduced whole orders of Christian knights into forbidden sexual practices, drugs, and even human sacrifice?

They have been credited on the one hand as the founders of the mysterious but benevolent fellowships of Knights Templars, Freemasonry, and Rosecrucianism. On the other bloody hand, the Order of Assassins has been cursed as the inspiration for a plethora of deadly secret societies and fanatical religious and political organizations both East and West since the Middle Ages. The cult has been cited as creators of the magician's staples of the "levitating body," Houdini's "metamorphosis," and sawing-the-woman-in-two illusions that, in the hands of the assassins, were harnessed to goals far more sinister than mere entertainment. What masterful combination of magical illusion, psychology, theatrics, and martial arts did the elusive grand masters of this cult of killers use to control disciples and terrorize enemies? Did their seemingly miraculous mental powers and unstoppable fighting prowess really flow from their addiction to the capricious "perfume of Heaven," hashish? Or, as many still believe, did the Assassin grand master possess real magical powers? Is it true they could predict the moment of a man's death by reading his stars; that they possessed the power to shape-shift into animal forms; that they had mastered the secret of the flying carpet; and that, before the collapse of their cult, they hid the cypher for this forbidden knowledge within the arcane symbolism of occult tarot cards?

More important still, is the Order of Assassins dead, or do their shadow-sons still lurk in the comforting dark, their poison-dipped daggers drawn and poised?

A word of warning is in order before we once more invade the East with crusader zeal, before we ask questions perhaps better left unasked. We must beware, thinking long and hard, before jerking aside the seven veils that obscure the Assassin's murderous world of smoke and mirrors—smoke no blade can cut, darkened mirrors designed to reflect back our own fear!

Before taking that first irreversible step, we must steel our will and prepare our mind to accept uncomfortable answer, lest, like so many unfortunates in the past, we awake one morning to a bed drenched in cold sweat, a darkly jeweled dagger buried in the pillow beside our head: a friendly reminder that we shouldn't ask questions we aren't fully prepared to pay the price for.

That is, if we wake up at all.

PART ONE

CHAPTER ONE

The Brotherhood of the Blood-Lickers

"Assassins. One never knew when they would strike, and there was nothing that could be done to scare them off. Indeed, when captured they went to their deaths eagerly, joyfully. How can one deal with men who do not fear death? What was the power the Old Man of the Mountain had over his followers that they obeyed his every wish without consideration of their own lives?"

—Barry Sadler,
Casca #13: The Assassin

STRATEGY AND STRONGHOLDS

The short version is this: In the late 11th century, Hasan ibn Sabbah, forced from his studies in Cairo, returned to his home in southern Persia, acquired a mountain fortress by hook or by crook, and created a cult of killers who terrorized the Middle East for centuries to come.

Strategy

Though dominated by Sunnis over a period of three centuries, Ismailis in Persia succeeded in establishing small semiautonomous enclaves in the Khuzistan region (north of the Arabian Sea, northeast of the Persian Gulf). Disappointed by the lack of enthusiasm shown for his ideas by the Ismaili leadership, Hasan was nonetheless determined to go forward with his plans.

Lacking both the wealth and well-equipped army he needed to wrest control of the Ismaili enclaves, Hasan set out to create a sect all his own, one consisting of a small, specially trained and trusted inner circle, insulated by a larger outer circle of general members whose job it was to give supply and succor to the inner circle elite.

Having established this support network, Hasan set about taking over the existing Ismaili infrastructure. Over a period of years, Hasan 's agents infiltrated not just the Ismaili leadership, but also the retinues of enemy potentates and notables, gathering intelligence, sowing distrust, waiting for the signal from the grand master to strike. Secret converts were made, shallow graves were dug. One by one, one way or another, opponents disappeared.

While a complex thinker, Hasan' s overall strategy was simple: All problems can be solved either through education or assassination. Opponents refusing to participate were treated to a fatal dose of the latter.

Quietly, patiently, Hasan extended his reach, applying this "education or assassination" for-mula.

Strongholds

"Mystic masters who perform satanic feats often retreat to such places where devils most often reside."

—Ibn Taymeeyah
as translated by Abu Ameenah Bilal Philips

Hasan needed a training camp where he could train and temper the faithful. He chose the near impregnable, centuries old Castle Alamut.

Set high on a 600-foot cliff in the remote Alamut River valley in the Elburz Mountains, Castle Alamut could be reached only by almost perpendicular steps crudely hacked out of rock. How Hasan acquired this castle is subject to debate. The simplest version is tha tHasan and his followers spent months secretly infiltrating the imposing castle and slowly converting the castle guards. Other versions have Hasan bribing the lord of the castle with 3000 gold dinars, threatening him, and making him a secret convert. The most interesting version sounds more like the sort of skullduggery Hasan was noted for: After Hasan saved the governor of the Alamut region from an assassin (a killer Hasan himself had sent), the governor insisted Hasan accept a reward. Hasan humbly responded that all he wanted was that portion of the governor's lands that could be encircled by Hasan 's green cloak. The governor quickly agreed.

The next day the governor awoke to discover that Hasan had unraveled his cloak and, tieing the threads together, had encircled the whole of Castle Alamut! Chagrined, but not wanting to look the fool, the governor kept his part of the bargain.

Whichever story is true, by 1090 Hasan and his followers had taken control of Castle Alamut. After obtaining the castle, Hasan and his followers then set about subverting and converting the region's populace. Through a masterful blend of proselytising, subterfuge, and force, Hasan's *dai* (agents) soon gained control of the towns and other fortresses in the area.

Safe in his eagle's nest at Alamut, it is estimated that Hasan had 70,000 of his followers strategically placed throughout the Middle East by 1092. Most important of these were agents sent to establish a Syrian branch of the Assassins in Aleppo. More on this influential Aleppine Assassin branch later.

The Cult and the Craft

Like the Grand Lodge of Cairo, Hasan's organization had both an overt cult message taught to the general membership, and a covert craft of subterfuge, intrigue, and murder taught to the elite.

The Cult

The main body of Hasan's overt teachings were derived from the Nizari splinter of the Ismaili branch of the Shiite split of the Islamic tree. The Nizari had their origin in yet another succession dispute within the Shiite community, which Hasan was able to take advantage of. Hasan freely incorporated teachings and rituals from traditions and religions other than orthodox Islam, not the least of which was the Ismailis' convoluted history:

"At this time Ismailism had existed for over three centuries and represented a broad spectrum of the discontented anti-Arab natives, oppressed peasants, dissatisfied

9

artisans, devout Muslims resenting the secularism and corruption of the age, and the believers in the millennium. It was at one and the same time a Shiite sect combining Islamic and pre-Islamic Greek, Persian, Syrian, and Babylonian concepts; an Alid [followers of All] secret society dedicated to the overthrow of the Sunnite Abbasids; and a revolutionary social movement pledged to improve the lot of the depressed. Nor did it limit itself to Muslims. Tending toward inter-confessionalism, it appealed to Jews, Christians, and Zarathustrans. Within the Abbasid Khalifate its missionary activities were perforce clandestine."

—Franzius

As a result:

"[Hasan's cult] was a compound of Magianism, Judaism, Christianity and Mohammedanism."

—Latham

Like his alma mater, the Grand Lodge at Cairo, Hasan's cult offered nine levels (degrees) of knowledge, beginning with overt orthodox Islamic teachings and through deepening levels leading toward a transcendence of all religion and reason other than the word of the grand master himself. At each level, the Assassin initiate drifted further away from orthodox Ismaili doctrine and more into cult worship of Imam Hasan. By the fifth degree, initiates had rejected any literal interpretation of the Quran and relied instead on the grand master's esoteric interpretations. At this level, initiates were also introduced to the pseudo-sciences of astrology, numerology, and various other occult practices. Level six initiates abandoned all overt Muslim observances (prayer, fasting, etc.) and entered the rankings of dai. Accepted agents then received specialized training as field agents (propagandists, spies, assassins).

Ninth degree initiates were inducted into the inner circle of the cult, which was also known as the Red Circle or the Red Mosque.

Hasan and this Inner Circle used all the hooks that cultists have always used to attract converts. Recruits were promised the chance to be one of "the chosen few," a chance to punish their oppressors and dispense justice, the removal of individual responsibility, freedom to do taboo things, and told that "secret" knowledge and powers would be revealed to the faithful. Hasan was aided in his recruitment by the still widespread pre-islamic beliefs in magic and demons.

MAGIC

The Muslim belief in magic has wavered little since the time of Muhammed. One modern authority on Islamic beliefs defines magic as:

". . . any phenomenon that has invisible causes or that is seen or imagined differently from its reality, due to disguise or trickery. Other scholars define magic more narrowly as the art of producing in nature, with the help of demons, things beyond the power of men. In fact, there are many types of magic, some are all illusions and trickery, others are real and occur with the help of the devil."

—al-Jumah

So widespread was the practice of magic (the use of spells, talismans, and charms, etc.) in the early days of Islam that Muslim leaders passed edicts and conducted wi tch hunts against such practices:

"Umar Ibn al-Khattab, the second Khalifah, ordered his governors to kill any magician in the Muslim territory, as they were considered disbelievers and harmful . . . For these reasons, sorcery was rarely practiced in the first centuries of Islam, but as the Muslim [union] became weaker, and as deviations and sins became a common feature of the Muslim communities, the practice of magic reappeared again."

—al-Jumah

In order to exploit this widespread belief in magic, Hasan

developed elaborate stage illusions (levitation, shape-shifting, escapology) designed to mimic "real" magic powers. Hasan also went out of his way to encourage any belief that he had been given magical powers from Jinn demons, or that he and his dai were actually Jinn in human form.

JINN

The word Jinn comes from the verb *janna*, which means "to hide." Jinn became "genie" in English. According to one authority on the subject:

> "The Jinn are beings created with free will, living on earth in a world parallel to that of men and are invisible to human eyes in their normal state."

> —Ibn Taymeeyah
> as translated by Abu Ameenah Bilal Philips

A Jinn may possess a man if invited by sensuous desire. At other times:

> "Demonic possession occurs as a result of horseplay, jest or plain evil on the part of the Jinn just as evil and mischief occurs among humans for similar reasons."

> —Ibn Taymeeyah
> as translated by Abu Ameenah Bilal Philips

Jinns were thought to dwell in shadowed valleys, a point not lost on Hasan as he sat in his castle in the valley of Alamut. Jinn were shape-shifters, able to take the form of animals, especially venomous ones such as snakes and scorpions. Jinn were tricksters who sometimes aided humans but most often tempted them. According to Islamic scholar Ibn Taymeeyah:

> "The evil Jinns reveal to their human allies hidden knowledge which the ignorant masses assume to be among the miracles given only to pious God-fearing saints, when in fact they are only Satanic deceptions manifest in the

devil's helper on whom is Allah's displeasure and who have gone astray."

—as translated by Abu Ameenah Bilal Philips

Like all cult leaders, Hasan encouraged superstitions that further added to his mystique and that of his agents. Often, the best cloak in which to wrap yourself is your enemy's superstition, the best of masks to hide behind, your enemy's fear! Potential Assassin converts were told that the green cloak Hasan always wore—the one he had unraveled to obtain Castle Alamut—was the same green cloak the prophet himself had used to lift the sacred black stone into place at the rebuilding of the Ka'ba; that Hasan' s followers were themselves descended from the blood-lickers who had bound themselves to death during the rebuilding of the Ka'ba; and that Hasan had been given secret knowledge and powers from the Jinn. Or maybe Hasan and his killers were Jinn in humam form!

This would not be the first nor the last time a killer cadre encouraged the superstitious awe of outsiders. Thuggee stranglers of India encouraged the belief that they were Bengal tigers transformed into men by the goddess Kali. The feared leopard cult of Africa spread the rumor that they were men possessed by the vengeful leopard spirit. And the dreaded ninja of Japan encouraged the belief that they were descended from tenyu, half-man, half-crow forest demons.

CRAFT

" . . . know ye that for him who follows the Way of the Hashishi death is but the opening portal into paradise, a foretaste of what will be yours on the other side of the tomb. And that ye may know the saying is true, put on now the robes of resurrection before you enter this tomb; drink now the elixir that promises Paradise before you enter the darkness. Come now, Hashishi!"

—Barry Sadler,
Casca #13: The Assassin

Often, much is said, when so little is certain. So much about

Hasan's secret society remains shrouded in mystery. Even the origin of its name is disputed. Crusaders took the word *assassin* back to Europe with them. Assassin is a corruption of *hashishin*, and refers to the widespread belief that Hasan doped his recruits up on hashish before sending them out on suicide missions. For those unfamiliar with hashish and its effects:

> "Hashish is the resin of the cannabis plant, which is removed by crushing and boiling the leaves and stems in water. The resulting residue when dried is a semisolid and can be smoked, chewed or mixed with food, as can any other form of marijuana. Hashish oil is obtained by extracting it from the plants with organic solvents. It has a very high THC content, up to 30 percent. It too can be eaten in food or sprinkled on tobacco or marijuana leaves and smoked."

—Duke & Gross

The effects of hashish range from a feeling of lackadaisical euphoria to one of fear—hardly the drug of choice for a killer. Hasan is also said to have used hashish to place recruits in a stupor before showing them his ersatz Garden of Paradise.

Marco Polo was the first to tell the tale of the Assassins' pleasure garden. The story goes that the recruits were first doped up with hashish—the "perfume of Heaven"—before being escorted to an idyllic hidden garden in the valley of Alamut where they were provided with all manner of forbidden pleasures such as food, wine, and sex. After hours or days spent in this garden, sobering recruits would awaken back at Castle Alamut, where then told that what they had experienced was but a foretaste of the paradise that awaited them, should they die in Hasan's service. Whether or not the Assassin cult actually used hashish to seduce recruits is a matter of debate.

The true origin of the word *assassin* was a misinterpretation of either Hashimite (persons having common ancestry with the prophet Muhammed; from Hashim, Muhammed's great-grandfather), or Hasanites, followers of Hasan. Given the suicidal dedication of the Hasanites, it is easy to understand how Europeans grasped at the idea that the only possible explanation for the feroc-

ASSASSIN RANKINGS

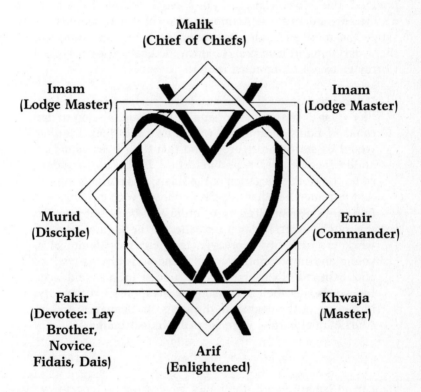

Malik
(Chief of Chiefs)

Imam
(Lodge Master)

Imam
(Lodge Master)

Murid
(Disciple)

Emir
(Commander)

Fakir
(Devotee: Lay
Brother,
Novice,
Fidais, Dais)

Khwaja
(Master)

Arif
(Enlightened)

Salik (Seeker)
Laziks (Uninitiated)
Rafig ("Friends")
Fidavis
Dayes

ity of the Assassins was that the killers were high on drugs. So far as needing a drug to trick his fidais into throwing away their lives, there was no need. Once a follower had reached the coveted degree of *fakir-dai*, he was ready to gladly die for the Order.

In our tepid age, it is as impossible for many people to understand the mindset of a suicide car-bomber as it is for them to comprehend the motivations of an ancient Viking *berserker*, the doomed defenders at the Alamo, or a World War II kamikaze pilot. While the motivation and politics of each of these differs, they share one thing in common: fanatical dedication to an ideal, to a worthy cause, or a respected leader:

> "Such was [Hasan's] fame and such the Ismailis' zeal that there was ever an excess of applicants for admission to the ranks of fidais, although it was known that their training would be stern and rigorous and that their lives would in all likelihood end early and in torture. In seeking to understand the stoic abnegation of the fidais, it is perhaps important to remember that they were chosen with circumspection, not only for strength of mind and body but also for that of character, and were expelled at the slightest sign of weakness or levity. Moreover, they entered Alamut at a young and impressionable age, some as young as twelve, and believed themselves to be under divine guidance. Indeed, beside their instruction in weaponry, particularly in the use of the dagger, in disguises, in languages, and in court etiquette, they were carefully indoctrinated."

—Franzius

For an Ismaili youth, the honor of wearing the coveted white tunic and red sash of the Assassin elite (the same colors as Knights Templars initiates, by the way) was comparable to a young soldier today earning the honor of wearing the coveted green beret of the Special Forces.

Merely to survive Assassin training was an accomplishment. Initiates were taught not only physical disciplines and killing craft, but also mental disciplines designed to focus the mind, which were mental gymnastics similar to Hindu yoga and meditation.

All aspects of initiate training involved risk and many trainees died before formal initiation. Even when a trainee made it to graduation, there was a chance of sudden death. In the Assassin initiation ceremony, 10 initiates would stand in a circle while the green-robed grand master walked counterclockwise around the outside of the circle. Former initiates stood in a larger outer circle, chanting. On his left hand the grand master wore a white glove. His black-gloved right hand gripped an ornate silver dagger said to be made from a silver nail once stuck in the wall of the secret tomb of the prophet. On cue, the chanting stopped and the grand master would plunge the dagger into the back of one of the initiates, killing him instantly. The rest were welcomed as full Brothers in Blood. In Assassin lore, the number nine is held to be sacred. A new circle (lodge) could only be founded by nine initiates. As we will see in the section on Assassin offshoots and imitators, much of the ritual and symbolism originated—or was at least pirated by—Hasan and passed into European freemasonry via the Knights Templars. For example:

"In Masonic symbolism the number nine is almost of unspeakable importance, and it represents the union of understanding of the material and spiritual."

—El-Amin

THE ART OF ASSASSINATION

Kill the brain of a snake and the most potent of venoms is rendered useless.

The idea of assassination offends our modern Western sensibilities. We are told that Western governments no longer sanction the assassination of foreign leaders, no matter how dangerous, no matter how loathesome. This policy has its origin not in practicality, but in the fear of Western politicians that they will be targeted in retaliation. These politicians know that there is a big difference between your sitting in a safe office and signing a paper to send soldiers off to die in foreign lands, and your having to personally worry about taking a bullet from a foreign country's assassin.

Historians speculate endlessly what the effect on world history might have been had an assassin's bullet or bomb succeeded in killing Hitler or Stalin prior to September 1, 1939. What would be the effect on the world tomorrow if a bullet or bomb got to

17

Ghaddafi or Saddam Hussein? Do the math. Are the lives of thousands or millions of war dead, soldiers and civilians alike, really equal to one troublesome Hitler, Stalin, or Hussein? According to Enno Franzius, in his *History of the Order of Assassins*:

> "Hasan's contribution to the art of assassination was that by careful selection, training, and inspiration he developed the practice into a sacred ritual and the prime weapon of a small state waging war against a great power. Thus, Alamut became the greatest training center for fanatical politico-religious assassins that the world has known."

Beyond mere revenge, Hasan's strategy was to employ the same kind of hit and run tactics used by guerrilla fighters the world over, from ninja to Vietcong, colonial minutemen to Navy SEALS:

> "Apart from the fact that it would have been folly to engage the numerically superior Sunnites in pitched battle, the Master's policy of assassination was a relatively bloodless way of waging war. One man—a potentate, a general, a governor, or an important minister—was killed instead of many in battle. Only as a last resort would the assassins engage in military operations and then generally on a small scale, such as the capture of a castle or the seizure of a town from within. Thus the murder of a general on the eve of a battle often determined its course, the killing of a key figure halted a project, or the assassination of an able man prevented the restoration of order and unity."

> —Franzius

Often, merely the threat of being targeted was enough. Remember that the Old Man of the Mountain's first choice for dealing with human obstacles was education:

> "Often the lord of Alamut could channel the course of history simply by a mysteriously placed message, significantly transfixed by a dagger."

> —Franzius

THE SELJUK-ASSASSIN WAR (1092-1118)

As a pro-Fatimid Shiite, Hasan's immediate enemy was the Abbasids and their Sunnite Seljuk overlords. Seljuks were Turks who came from central Asia in the 11th century to establish an empire stretching from the borders of India to the Mediterranean Sea. Seljuks adopted Arab culture, championed their own particular brand of Sunnite Islam, and imposed rule over minority Kurdish and Persian Shiites.

The October 1092 assassination of Hasan's former friend—and betrayer?—Nizam al-Mulk, grand vizier to the Seljuk Sultan Malik Shah, was not the first assassination by Hasan's newly formed cadre of killers, but Nizam 's death must have brought especial satisfaction to Hasan. Nizam's killing also brought the wrath of the Seljuks down on the heads of the Order of Assassins. In retaliation for the death of his grand vizier, Malik Shah launched what would become a protracted 30-year assault against Alamut. Retaliation had been expected. Hasan had fortified the already inaccessible Alamut, but had no intention of fighting a purely defensive war against the Seljuks.

In November 1092, while listening to the latest excuses from frustrated commanders beseiging Alamut, Malik Shah drank Assassin poison and dropped dead. His death temporarily terminated Seljuk operations against Alamut. More importantly, the deaths of Nizam and Malik—within two months of one another—threw centralized Seljuk power into chaos. Power slipped into the hands of regional Seljuk rulers, who immediately split into warring factions over the question of who should rule after Malik Shah. As Hasan had expected, this successional infighting further weakened Seljuk influence in Persia and Iraq.

Playing one Seljuk upstart off against another—some ambitious Seljuk upstarts even hired Assassins to kill rival Seljuks—Hasan took advantage of the disorder to seize and fortify additional Assassin strongholds in the Elbruz mountains, in Khuzistan, and in the mountains between Fars and Khuzistan:

"No doubt Hasan strove to prolong and profit from the confusion resulting from the Seljuks failure to create a unitary state [after the death of Malik Shah]."

—Franzius

19

By 1105 Sultan Muhammed Tapar had wrested control of the Seljuk realm and once again Seljuks undertook major expeditions to drive the Assassins from their strongholds. Tapar used the real and imagined threat posed by the Assassins as a rallying cry, uniting the Seljuks. Tapar besieged Castle Alamut, devastated the countryside, and slaughtered Ismaili converts in droves. Secure inside Alamut, Hasan and his Inner Circle held out with a small cadre of only 72 men—the number is probably symbolic—until reinforced by a few hundred Ismailis from the area. Finally, a night assault on the Sultan's camp by Assassin sappers broke Tapar's siege. Various Seljuk commanders made several other attempts take Alamut, but all failed.

Other Assassin strongholds were not as fortunate, however. A force of 80 Assassins occupying the largely demolished fortress of Shadiz held out for weeks against a vastly superior Seljuk force. In a scene later pirated by the film *Beau Geste*, to give impression they were more numerous, the Assassin defenders placed weapons in the hands of propped-up dead comrades. Unable to get reinforcements, most of the Shadiz Assassins died fighting or leaped to their deaths from the high castle walls rather than be captured. Those few captured were flayed alive.

The Seljuk-Assassin War continued. A classic study in guerrilla warfare, Hasan's fists thrust out from Alamut and other Assassin strongholds, striking down Seljuk targets and quickly withdrawing before caught by numerically superior forces.

In September 1106, the grand vizier of Khurasan was stabbed to death by an Assassin disguised as a beggar. Captured and tortured, the Assassin revealed 12 co-conspirators, all Seljuk loyalists. The Seljuk traitors were executed side-by-side with the captured Assassin. Only later were all the courtiers discovered to be innocent.

It is a moot point whether the captured Assassin knew he was giving false names or, spotting an inherent character flaw in their agent, expecting that he would break under torture, Assassin controllers gave the Assassin a list of false contacts. The fact remains:

" . . . with a single dagger thrust the fidai had sent thirteen men to the grave."

—Franzius

In November of 1109, Ahmed, grand vizier of the Sultan and son of Nizam al-Mulk, was crossing the Tigris at Baghdad when his boat was boarded by an Assassin who plunged a knife into his neck, paralyzing him.

Finally, in April of 1118, Sultan Tapar himself drops dead. Assassins had made several unsuccessful attempts to kill Tapar, but history records Tapar died of natural causes. However, Middle Eastern and later European governments often listed successful murders committed by the Assassins as "natural causes," lest confidence in the government's ability to combat Hasan's terrorists be undermined.

Sultan Tapar was succeeded by Sanjar, son of Malik Shah. Sanjar loudly declared his deter-mination to carry on the Seljuk war against the Assassins, that is, until he awoke one morning in his campaign tent to find a dagger on his pillow along with a note from the Old Man of the Mountain requesting that Sanjar send envoys to Castle Alamut for negotiations.

First the envoys were feasted, then, in a demonstration of his power, the grand master had one Fidai cut his own throat and a second hurl himself to death off Alamut's high walls. Hasan casually informed the shocked envoys that he had 60,000 such Assassins prepared to likewise sacrifice themselves in the Assassin cause, i.e., killing Seljuks. When terror-stricken envoys relayed this to their Sultan, Sanjar agreed to withdraw troops from Assassin territory and agreed to pay tribute to the Assassin chief. In return, Hasan agreed not to proselytize in Sultan's domain. The Seljuk-Assassin War was over.

Hasan lived 34 years after taking Alamut. He had sacrificed much to establish his dream, and had suffered persecution and imprisonment. On several occasions he had barely escaped the executioner's axe. He had survived numerous attempts on his own life, several from fellow Ismailis, and had spent years of hardship traveling, culling the chosen from the frozen. Then came years in hiding, shaping and sharpening the weapons of his will. To safeguard his dream, Hasan even had his own two sons killed for violating the rules of the Order—one for drunkenness, the other for carrying out an unauthorized assassination. Yes, the Old Man of the Mountain had sacrificed much for his dream. Now, as he lay dying, his plans for the continuence of the Order firmly in place, the Old Man of the Mountain smiled, knowing that his dream would one day become the world's nightmare.

CHAPTER TWO

Grand Masters and Grand Schemes

"Although the Crusades were a military failure, western Europe was profoundly affected by the prolonged contact with the East, and both culture and trade were stimulated."

—*The New American Desk Encyclopedia*

THE CRUSADERS

Any reader who thinks the Middle Ages in general, and the Crusades in particular, are dry history needs to realize that the Crusades are the bloody medieval background against which political ploys and power plays were made and shady deals and unholy alliances forged (that we are still feeling the effects of and still paying the price for). The Crusades were not just Christians vs. Muslims, but Christian vs. Christian, Muslim vs. Muslim, and Mongols vs. everybody. Within each crusading army, contentious warlords vied for the upper hand. Within every sect and religious order, internecine warfare and treachery was the order of the day as rival fanatics slew heretical brethren.

The Middle East during the Middle Ages was ripe for the taking by any ambitious warlord with a rusty sword and every manipulating cult leader with a good line of bull.

As in any important historical period, during the Crusades we find players both pivotal and peripheral, each maneuvering for a

23

better angle from which to cut his rival's throat. And listening behind every curtain, ready with a perfidious whisper or a poisoned dagger, Hasan's cult of Assassins, although sometimes caught in the middle, were more often than not playing both ends against the middle. By studying the triumphs and tragedies of these players, their motivations and hidden agendas will help us to better understand the motivations and hidden agendas of today's Middle Eastern players and slayers.

THE CRUSADES

The Crusades were a series of military campaigns undertaken by European kingdoms, which were aimed at recovering Christian holy places in Palestine. Islam had threatened Europe for hundreds of years, but internecine fighting between rival European kings had prevented any concerted effort to combat the encroaching Muslims:

> Lacking leadership and beset by raids, Europe could barely hold the Muslims in check. When the destructive raids of the [Viking] Northmen ended in the High Middle Ages (1050-1270), European monarchs could begin to weld feudal lands into kingdoms. The population was increasing and the economy growing. Late in the eleventh century the West became strong enough to take the offensive against Islam.
>
> Marvin Perry,
> *Unfinished Journey: A World History*

By 1071, advancing Seljuk Turks had taken Jerusalem and were threatening the West Roman-Byzantine Empire, so Pope Urban II called for a "holy crusade" to take back the Holy Land. Beyond mere piety, Pope Urban II had several reasons for calling for a mass mobilization against the Muslims, not the least of which was strengthening the power of the Vatican. As Perry puts it: "Instead of warring among themselves, lords were fighting together with the Pope as their leader. This strengthened papal power."

Crusading also appealed to Europe's royalty. It cost a lot of money to maintain feudalism, and raping the Holy Land held the promise of booty. Europe's feudal laws of primogeniture, whereby only eldest sons inherited lands, produced a surplus of young men—princes and lesser nobles—with a lot of idle time on their hands to plot against their elder brothers. Crusading offered the opportunity that the more Machiavellian of these princes might carve out kingdoms of their own in the Holy Land.

Over a period of 200 years, from the 11th to the 13th century, nine major crusades were undertaken by Europeans, with degrees of success ranging from victory to fiasco. The First Crusade (1095-1099), composed of four large European armies, drove the Seljuk Turks off the Asia Minor peninsula before thrusting down into the Levant (modern-day Lebanon, Syria, and Israel).

By 1100 European crusaders had established the "Four Crusader Kingdoms" in the Levant: the Fiefs of Tripoli, Antioch, and Edessa and the Latin kingdom of Jerusalem, which included the strategic cities of Jaffa, Ramleh, and Galilee.

The Turkish recapture of Edessa in 1144 incited the Second Crusade (1147-1148). Led by rivals Louis VII of France and Conrad III of Germany, their attack against Damascus failed because of their mutual jealousy. Muslims recaptured Jerusalem in 1187, provoking Holy Roman Emperor Frederick I, Phillip II of France, and Richard I of England to launch the Third Crusade (1189-1192). Disunited by rivalry, this federation of Christians failed to wrest Jerusalem away from the Muslims. However, on his own, Richard I ("Richard the Lionhearted") succeeded in seizing several coastal towns, including the strategic town of Acre. Richard shocked and angered many by making a separate truce with Muslim warlord Saladin, a truce guaranteeing Christian pilgrims safe passage through the Holy Land.

During the Fourth Crusade (1201-1204), European crusaders heading to Palestine lost their road map and ended up sacking Constantinople (Istanbul) instead.

The Fifth Crusade (1218-1221), the last launched with overt papal blessing, was a botched invasion of Egypt, aborted after Christian crusaders were trapped by floodwaters near Cairo.

The Sixth Crusade (1228-1229) brought Jerusalem under control of Holy Roman Emperor Frederick II, but by 1244, Jerusalem was again in Muslim hands.

The Seventh Crusade (1248-1254), led by France's Louis IX, was a crowning success, from the Muslim standpoint—Louis was captured by Muslims in Egypt. Ransomed and released and still not having learned his lesson, Louis launched the Eighth Crusade in 1270 but, mercifully, spared everybody involved further embarrassment by dropping dead at Tunis of plague or poison. Finally, in 1291, 200 years after Pope Urban's original call, Muslims recaptured Acre, the last Christian outpost in the Near East. Although sporadic free enterprise forays into the Middle East were made by groups of European mercenaries in the years following, there were no further large-scale European crusades.

Results of the Crusades

In the end, the Crusades did succeed in strengthening papal power and helped unify kingdoms (if only by killing off superfluous princes and an excess of ambitious nobles). For better or worse, the Crusades also helped undermine Europe's basic social structure: feudalism.

Many a nobleman lost his fortune during the Crusades. Some crusading princes had borrowed heavily in order to foot their armies. When the dreamed-of riches failed to materialize, many of these nobles found themselves in debt to European money lenders. Conversely, the Crusades increased Europe's overall trade with the Middle East. Increased trade also hastened the decline of feudalism by encouraging the rise of bigger cities. These led to a rise of a middle class composed of merchants and guildsmen.

Christian Crusaders

Pope Urban's call for liberating the Holy Land had been met with enthusiasm, not just from nobles, but from commoners who saw crusading as their only chance to break the bonds of feudal servitude.

In the heady days of the First Crusade, groups of peasants and commoners, fired up by popular preachers, formed ill-equipped and poorly organized armies that marched off to the Holy Land. Looting their way across eastern Europe, one such band massacred thousands of Jews in eastern Europe before being wiped out. Another of these commoner armies reached Asia Minor before being slaughtered by the Turks.

European merchants and money lenders likewise sponsored groups of mercenary knights for "free enterprise" pillaging forays to the east and into the Holy Land. When Pope Urban's call for crusaders went out, young knights

and would-be warriors, high on the ideal of achieving glory
in chivalrous battle, began champing at the bit. As a result,
"Eager for glory, adventure, wealth, and a chance to serve
God, lords and knights began to organize armies."

Marvin Perry,
Unfinished Journey: A World History

Each European kingdom had long maintained a cadre of
knights, but the time of the Crusades saw something new: the rise
of universal knights orders, sanctioned by and answerable only to
the Vatican. Many European rulers feared the idea of these "international" knights orders, since young men, many of them nobles,
who joined these orders came from all over Europe and had to put
aside petty nationalist loyalties and intrigues in favor of serving the
Vatican and/or the aims of the international orders.

Knights Templars
One of these "universal" orders of knights was the *militia tem-
pli*: the "Soldiers of Solomon's Temple." Better known as the
Knights Templars, this order of warrior-monks was founded in
1118 by nine knights under Grand Master Hugh dePayens. Initially
a poor order, they chose as their emblem two knights riding a single horse. Their vows held them to poverty and valor, and their
commission was to protect pilgrims traveling in the Holy Land.

Templars recruiters traveled across France and England signing up young warriors. Richard the Lionhearted, impressed by the
Templars vow to stand their ground against 3-to-1 odds, supported
them. When the Count of Anjou gave up his noble robes for the
spartan white tunic of the Templars, his example was soon followed by other Western princes.

In 1127 the Knights Templars were recognized as an official
order by the Pope. King Baldwin II of Edessa offered their order
part of his palace for their headquarters so, in 1129, the Templars
grand master and 300 Knights Templars recruited from the noblest
houses in Europe led a huge train of pilgrims to the Holy Land.

In 1133, King Alfonso of Aragon and Navarre (southern
France, northern Spain) willed his entire country to the Templars
order. The catch was that the area was still in Moor-controlled territory. Gradually, Knights Templars were either willed or purchased or captured forts and lands in the Holy Land. As was the

custom of the day, Templars provided "protection" to the people in territories under their order's control in return for those people paying a regular tribute tax.

As a result of town and territory seizures, gifts, and tribute, within a short time the Order of Knights Templars grew wealthy and powerful and were soon influencing European politics. In 1154 two rival popes were elected: Alexander III, backed by a powerful faction of Sicilians, and Victor III, backed by an imperial party composed of the Holy Roman Emperor and other kings. At first the Templars acknowledged Victor III, but in 1161 they switched to Alexander III, insuring his acceptance as the legitimate pope. In exchange for their support, in 1162 Alexander III issued a declaration making Templars answerable only to the Holy See. In addition, Templars were declared exempt from paying tithes but could still receive tribute from lands under their control. In effect, this papal bull made the Templars equivalent to an autonomous state. It also made the Templars many envious enemies.

Knights Hospitallers

Bitter rivals of the Templars, the Order of the Hospital of St. John of Jerusalem—Knights Hospitallers—had received a papal charter in 1113 for the purpose of tending sick pilgrims in the Holy Land. By 1161, however, the Knights Hospitallers had grown into a private army, having carved themselves a respectable piece of the Middle Eastern pie by seizing several strongholds and exhorting tribute from the people in areas controlled by them. They were knee deep in Middle Eastern slaughter and skullduggery. Given the lucrative operation Knights Hospitallers had going, it is understandable that they should view as a threat the rise of the Knights Templars.

There is ample evidence that Knights Hospitallers were either in secret alliance with the Order of Assassins or, at the very least, contracted the Assassins on several occasions to assassinate Hospitaller enemies. When Adam of Baghras, Regent of Antioch, was killed, Knights Hospitallers were accused of having contracted the Assassins to do the deed, but the pope refused to investigate reports of a Hospitallers-Assassin alliance. In 1213, Raymond, eldest son of King Bohemond of Antioch, was visiting the Knights Templars at Tortosa when he was attacked and stabbed by several Assassins. King Bohemond and the Knights Hospitallers had been at odds for a long time, and the patriarch of Jerusalem openly accused the Hospitallers of paying for Raymond's murder. Shortly thereafter, as if in confirmation, the patriarch himself was murdered by Assassins.

In response, Bohemond and the Templars besieged the Assassin stronghold of Khawal until the Sunnite Emir of Aleppo, under threat by the Assassins, persuaded Bohemond and the Templars to withdraw.

Muslim Crusaders

At the time of the First Crusade, Islam was divided into the Seljuk-Sunnite Caliph based in Baghdad and the Fatimid-Shiite Caliph based in Egypt. According to John J. Robinson in his *Dungeon, Fire & Sword*, it was warring between these Shiites and Sunnis that made the European victories of the First Crusade possible. European diplomacy and double-dealing would continue to play one against the other until the coming of Saladin.

Islamic infighting also allowed Muslim "crusaders" and warlords to assert themselves; some for Islam, some for personal empire.

Taking advantage of Seljuk disunity, the Egyptian warlord Nur ed-Din and his Mamelukes pushed north from Egypt, expanding his domains, taking Damascus in 1154 and Mosul in 1170. Nur ed-Din was aided in his conquests by two able generals: Prince Mleh of Armenia and Saladin. Prince Mleh was a renegade Templars. After being passed over for the throne of Armenia by his brother, Prince Mleh converted to Catholicism in order to join the Templars. Discovered to be behind a plot to assassinate his brother, Prince Mleh fled to the court of Nur ed-Din, converted to Islam, and was given command of Nur ed-Din's Turkish cavalry. Proving the worth of Templars training, Prince Mleh took the Armenian principality of Cilicia and captured the towns of Tarsus, Adana, and Mamistra for Nur ed-Din before sweeping south toward Antioch to lay siege to his former Templars comrades' castle at Baghras. Mleh was finally forced to retreat in the face of Templars reinforcements. In 1174 Nur ed-Din died of disease or poison, and this led to the rise of Salah-ad-Din Yusuf ibn-Ayyub, known to Europeans as Saladin (1138-1193). Arguably the greatest military mind Islam ever produced, it was Saladin who crushed, once and for all, any dream of a Christian crusader empire in Palestine.

With the death of Nur ed-Din, several groups and principalities formally under his control revolted; however, Nur ed-Din's forces backed Saladin when he seized power in Cairo. Despite a formidable array of Syro-Mesopotamian Sunnites, Shiites, Latin crusaders, and Assassins all united against him, by April 1175 Saladin was in control of most of northern Syria. Unable to counter Saladin in open combat, the Regent of Aleppo hired Sinan, grand master of the Syrian Assassins, to kill Saladin. Shortly thereafter, a group of Assassin fidais slipped into Saladin's camp and killed a visiting emissary whom Saladin had graciously insisted spend the night in his tent, in his bed. Saladin escaped harm. In May 1176, while besieging Aza (northwest of Aleppo), Saladin, alone in his tent, was attacked by three Assassins, all trusted members of his bodyguard! An officer coming to Saladin's aid was wounded and the three Assassins killed, but Saladin again escaped harm. In August 1176, Saladin advanced on Masyaf (southwest of Kadmus). As he passed beneath a large tree, an Assassin leaped from overhanging branches, but was killed by Saladin's bodyguard. Again, Saladin escaped without a scratch.

In April 1183, Saladin sacked Aleppo and, to everyone's surprise, instead of punishing the Assassin sect for their numerous attempts on his life, Saladin made a deal whereby he agreed to leave Assassin lands and property intact. In return, Sinan agreed to stop assassination attempts against Saladin and even agreed to provide Saladin's army with Assassin troops.

Each assassination attempt Saladin survived increased the widespread belief that he was *chosen* by Allah. In order to foster this belief, it is widely believed that Saladin made a secret pact with Sinan wherein the Assassin chief would deliberately send compromised agents against Saladin; attackers Saladin could easily defend against. Whatever the truth of the matter, from 1183 on, Assassin "special forces" troops fought in Saladin's army as sappers and as a specific counterthreat to Knights Hospitallers and Templars.

By all accounts, Saladin hated Templars, whom he accused of being truce-breakers. When Saladin captured grand master Gerard of Ridefort and several Templars at the siege of Hittin in 1187, he ordered them all beheaded. Ironically, one of Saladin's best commanders, Robert St. Albans, was a renegade English Templars who had left the Order, become a Muslim, and led forces for Saladin against the French in Jerusalem. In 1187, when Saladin took Jerusalem, he was aided by Assassin sapper-infiltrators.

In August of 1192, Saladin and Richard the Lionhearted signed their infamous treaty ending the Third Crusade, leaving Christians the coastal cities as far south as Jaffa. On March 3, 1193, Saladin fell ill—from poison?—and died. His mighty empire fell apart within weeks of his death.

While just as many Muslims as Christians rejoiced at the death of Saladin, their celebration was short-lived. A new, more ominous threat loomed on the horizon. Both Christian and Muslim crusaders were about to encounter a horde of "crusaders" more forceful and more fanatical than themselves; fighters with no concept of Christian chivalry and no patience with Islam. More importantly, the Order of Assassins was about to be run up against a group of killers even more ruthless, more blood-thirsty than themselves!

MONGOLS

In 1194 a young warrior named Temujin, having succeeded where none before him had in uniting the warring Mongol clans of central Asia, took the title Genghis Khan ("Lord of Lords"). By 1215, Genghis Khan's huge, well-disciplined, and swift-moving horde had conquered northern China, was pushing through southern Russia into the Middle East, and was licking its lips every time it looked west toward Europe proper. Mongol conquests continued even after Genghis Khan's death in 1227. In 1251 Genghis' son Hulagu took Persia and gave his brother Jagatai control over Turkestan and Persia, including the Assassins' territory around Alamut. When Jagatai failed to show any interest in being "educated" in the Assassin way of thinking, Assassins killed him.

Enraged at his bother's murder, Hulagu ordered the Assassin sect wiped out. Hulagu himself led the punitive force of Mongols that swept across Assassin-held territory, crushing Assassin fortresses, killing every human being in every Assassin town and fortress taken. In order to accomplish his pogrom against the Assassin sect, Hulagu sent word that a census was being held. When rural families and Assassin supporters assembled, all were butchered. With Alamut in danger of falling, reigning Assassin Grand Master Khurshah quickly apologized for his predecessor's "rash" killing of Jagatai. Playing for time, Khurshah asked for and received permission from Hulagu to travel to the Mongol capital under a flag of truce for the purpose of petitioning Hulagu's brother Mongu, the ruling Khan, to pardon the Assassin sect. Hulagu agreed.

History records that the Assassin grand master and his entire party were subsequently ambushed and killed by the Mongols. The only Assassins to escape immediate death were those relatives of Grand Master Khurshah turned over to Jagatai's widow for her personal torture. But was the Assassin sect so easily destroyed?

We'll examine this more in a moment.

CHAPTER THREE

Ploys and Power Plays

In May 1121, Master Hasan ibn-Sabbah, in failing health, appointed his loyal emir, commander Buzurg-Umid, to succeed him as head of the Order of Assassins. In 1101, Umid had proved his military savvy by capturing the Castle of Lamasar, thus securing the approach to the Alamut valley. Umid then proved his dedication to the Old Man of the Mountain by systematically slaughtering all in the Alamut area who dared reject Hasanism. An able leader and strategist, Umid ruled the Assassin order from 1124-1138, carrying out his dead master's will, figuratively and literally. Umid's ruthlessness rivaled that of Hasan. For example, when two Assassin supporters were murdered by a mob in Isfahan, Umid butchered 400 citizens in retaliation. Thinking the Assassin order weakened by the death of the feared Old Man of the Mountain, in 1126 Seljuk Turk leader Sanjar launched a new offensive against the Alamut region. However, under Umid's leadership, the Assassins not only once more beat back the Turks, but succeeded in bringing new territory under Assassin control. Realizing his resolve as grand master was being tested, Umid went on the offensive, sending all Assassin enemies a clear message.

In March of 1127, Sanjar's Grand Vizier was killed by two Assassin *sleeper* agents posing as grooms. In November of 1130, 10 assassins ambushed and fatally wounded the Khalif of Cairo while he was on his way to visit a concubine. In 1135, taking advantage of the fact that one of their enemies had captured another of their enemies, Umid sent 10 Assassin sappers to infiltrate a heavily guarded camp where the Abbasid Khalif, Mustarshid, was being held for ransom by the Seljuks. After killing his guards, the Assassins stabbed Mustarshid 25 times, slit open his abdomen, cut off his nose, and decapitated him. As a final insult, departing assassins make a symbolic show of trampling on Mustarshid's corpse on their way out the door. All 10 Assassins are eventually cut down by Seljuk troops. Three years later, in Isfahan, Mustarshid's son Rashid was killed by Assassin sleeper agents who had infiltrated his court. It didn't take long for the enemies of the Assassin sect to realize that Hasan ibn-Sabbah might be dead, but it was business as usual so far as Umid, the *new* Old Man of the Mountain, was concerned.

As adept at skullduggery as he was at slaughter, one of Umid's most ambitious schemes involved a secret deal he made with King Baldwin II of Jerusalem in 1128. Their plan called for the Grand Vizier of Baghdad, an Assassin supporter, to open the gates of the city to Baldwin's Christian crusaders. In exchange, Baldwin agreed to give the Assassins control of the fortified city of Tyre. The plot was discovered, however, and the grand vizier and 10,000 suspected Assassin supporters in Baghdad were massacred.

Under Umid's leadership, the Order of the Assassins flourished. After Umid, the Order went straight to Hell.

GRAND (AND NOT SO GRAND) MASTERS

Umid was succeeded by his son Muhammad I, who ruled as Assassin grand master from 1138-1162. Muhammad's elevation to Grand master led to open rebellion within Assassin ranks. Many accused Umid of trying to establish a bloodline dynasty and openly challenged Muhammad's right to succeed his father. Graciously, Muhammad agreed to meet and discuss grievances with all those within the sect who opposed his leadership. When 500 challengers to his rule assembled for the meeting, Muhammad had his loyal troops kill the first 250 and then tie their corpses to the backs of the second 250, whom he then drove from Alamut.

Muhammad I ruled as grand master for 24 years without any further internal challenge to his leadership. He was succeeded by his son, Hasan II, who ruled for four very long years, 1162-1166. Also known as "Hasan the Mad," Hasan II removed Islamic ritual obligations from the Assassin sect, even to the point of permitting

ASSASSIN GRAND MASTERS

Hasan ibn-Sabbah (1050-1124: Founder)
|
Kia Buzurg-Umid 1124-1138)
|
Kia Muhammed (1138-1163: son of Umid)
|

Under Hasan the Hated, the Order of Assassins split into Alamut-Persian and Aleppo-Syrian branches. Hasan II ruled in Persian until he was assassinated and the Persian branch of the Order suppressed.

Hasan II (1163-1167: son of   **Sinan the Physician (1193)**
|

Muhammed I)
|
Muhammed II (1167-1191)
|
Prince Jalaludin (1191-1203)
|
Aladdin (1203: only 9 years old)
|
Rukneddim (1256: killed by Mongols?)
|
Baibars (1260: de facto Assassin grand master)

the consumption of alcohol (forbidden to Muslims, a taboo Hasan ibn-Sabbah, you will recall, had killed one of his own sons for breaking). Hasan the Mad also made public secret doctrines formally restricted to the elite Red Circle and declared himself the long-awaited Mahdhi, the Shiite messiah. Hasan's bizarre behavior, open debauchery, and orgies led to dissension within the Order of Assassins resulting in a split between Persian-Alamutine Assassins and the Aleppine branch of the sect centered in Aleppo, Syria.

Sinan and the Aleppine Assassins

In 1106, Hasan ibn-Sabbah dispatched trusted Emir Tahir ("The Goldsmith") to Syria to establish a "branch office" for the order. Tahir was a typically efficient assassin commander and did much to establish a permanent assassin presence in Syria. One of Tahir's many successful operations involved the seizure of the walled city of Apamea for the order. The first part of Tahir's plan called for six Assassin operatives to gain entrance to the city by ingratiating themselves with the town's ruler. To accomplish this, the operatives brought the ruler of Apamea the horse and weapons of a Christian crusader they claimed to have killed. Impressed, the ruler took the operatives into his service and gave them quarters in his citadel, conveniently next to the wall of the city. Later that night, the six infiltrators burrowed through the town's wall from the inside, admitting more Assassin sappers. The Assassins then slipped into the citadel's sleeping quarters and systematically slaughtered the ruler, his family, and his bodyguards. By morning, the Assassins had secured the city in the name of their commander, Tahir.

Although the Syrian branch of the Assassins made separate alliances and engaged secret allies over the years, the Aleppine Assassins continued to take their marching orders from Alamut, at least up until the time of Hasan the Mad. During the period of the First Crusade, Assassins in Syria allied themselves with Ridwan, the Seljuk ruler of Aleppo, against Ridwan's rival, Atabeg Janah al-Dawlah. Ridwan offered the Aleppine Assassins autonomy in exchange for the death of Janah.

In May of 1103, Atabeg Janah and several of his command staff were attacked and killed while observing mandatory Friday prayers in a mosque near Tripoli. (To gain entrance, the assassins disguised themselves as Sufi holy men.) Then, in December of

1113, Ridwan, patron and ally of the Assassins, was murdered. The son of Ridwan, believing the Assassin sect responsible, moved against them, executing Tahir and other leaders and exiling thousands of Assassin supporters from Aleppo.

The new leader of the Syrian Assassins, Bahram, made allies with Tughtengin, Regent of Damascus. Assassins sealed the pact in September 1113 by assassinating Tughtengin's foe, the Seljuk Emir of Mosul. In 1125, Assassins came to the aid of Tughtengin when Damascus was threatened by Crusaders. In appreciation, Tughtengin installed Assassin ambassadors and advisors in Damascus.

In 1129, Tughtengin's son and successor, Buri, discovering Grand Master Umid's plan to betray Damascus to the Christians, turned on the Assassins, slaying the pro-Assassin grand vizier and initiating the slaughter of upwards of 10,000 Assassin supporters in Damascus. Fearing reprisals after the Damascus massacre, Buri never left his palace except under heavy guard.

Finally, in May 1131, Assassins who had infiltrated his bodyguard attacked and mortally wounded Buri as he was leaving his bath.

By 1140 the Syrian branch of the Assassins were operating from a near autonomous territory with its center in the wild Ansarias Range, bordered by the Orontes River west to the Mediterranean coast, Antioch to the north, and Beirut to the south. Between 1132 and 1140 the Assassins gained control of several castles and strategic towns in this area. Some they purchased, such as Kadmus and Kahf; others, Khariba and Masyaf, they conquered from crusaders or from brother Muslims, respectively.

In 1162, shortly after the ascension of Hasan the Mad as Alamut's grand master, Sheikh Rashid ed-Din Sinan, chief Imam at the castle of Kahf in Syria, became the leader of the Aleppine Assassins. As chief Assassin at Kahf, Sinan, also known as "The Physician" for his mastery of poisons, had already proven his leadership ability. Realizing that superior intelligence—both the innate and the gathered varieties—equals success, Sinan directed his attention to creating a vast network of agents throughout the whole of Asia, which he then tied together using an efficient carrier-pigeon message system that winged vital information to the Assassin master much quicker and more efficiently than the other methods of the day. Through information provided him by his vast spy network and his expeditious messenger system, Sinan fostered the belief that he possessed an all-seeing eye. (Some even whispered that Sinan was the reincarnation of Hasan ibn-Sabbah.) Sinan encouraged both these superstitions. As we will see in a later section on psychological warfare, Sinan was a master manipulator who perfected illusions and mind manipulation techniques created by Hasan ibn-Sabbah and, in many cases, invented new techniques and illusions designed to convince the gullible that he possessed true magical powers. (The talking head ploy, so vital in the indictment and fall of the Knights Templars, was credited to Sinan.)

Initially, Sinan remained loyal to Hasan the Mad, but as Hasan's changes in the order became increasingly bizarre and his sympathy for

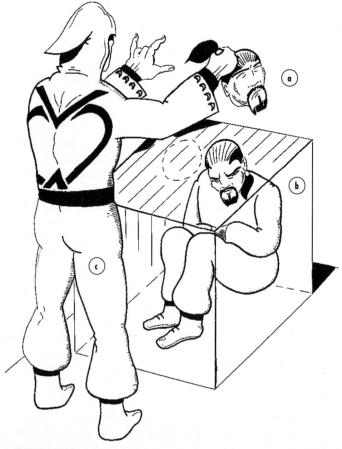

The "talking head" illusion.

the unique needs and situation of the Syrian branch became more apparent, Sinan began ignoring babblings from Alamut. Between 1162 and 1193, Sinan the Physician autonomously operated his own Aleppo-based Assassin sect from Alamut. Both Hasan and his successor, Muhammad II, sent Assassins to Aleppo to kill Sinan. Some of these Assassins died attempting to kill Sinan, but others defected to him. Unable to count on Alamut for support, Sinan needed allies to first counter the threat posed by Egyptian warlord Nur ed-Din and, second, the Knights Templars, who were bleeding tribute from Assassin supporters. In 1174, King Amalric I of Jerusalem, Baldwin's brother and heir to the throne, received an unexpected visit from the leader of the Syrian Assassins, who made Amalric an offer he couldn't refuse.

Sinan proposed an alliance between Amalric and the Assassins against Nur ed-Din. The Assassins would provide intelligence on Nur ed-Din's forces, as well as Assassin sappers should Amalric need them. In addition, Sinan would train a select cadre of Amalric's own troops in the tactics and techniques of the Assassins. To sweeten the pot, Sinan hinted that his branch of the Assassin sect might convert to Christianity en masse. Knowing the Assassins were fierce and fearless fighters and had the best intelligence network in Syria, Amalric agreed to the alliance. For his part, Amalric was obligated to come to the sect's aid should any of their strongholds come under siege by Nur ed-Din. Amalric also ordered the Templars grand master to cease bleeding annual tribute tax from Assassin families living in Templars-controlled territory.

This didn't sit too well with the Templars. In response, Templars Grand Master de St. Amand ordered the Assassins' emissaries ambushed and slain. Angered by the Templars defiance, Amalric demanded the Templars turn over the Templars responsible. When the Templars refused, Amalric forced his way into Templars residences and seized the offending knights. In addition to his dealings with the Christians, it was widely believed that Sinan made a secret deal with Nur ed-Din's general, Saladin.

When Nur ed-Din dropped dead of disease in 1174, whispers suggested that Saladin, a Kurd, had paid "the Physician" to poison the Egyptian Nur ed-Din. Sinan's alliances, overt and covert, first with Christians and then with Saladin, helped insure the survival and prosperity of the Aleppine Assassins until his death of natural causes in 1193. After the death of Sinan, the Aleppine Assassins again came under direct control of Alamut.

STRANGE BEDFELLOWS

"There is no good in much of their secret conferences. . ."

—The Quran

The only thing worse than having no suspect in a murder is having too many. Whenever an assassination took place in the Middle East during the Middle Ages, there was always an overabundance of suspects. Take, for example, the assassination of Count Raymond II of Tripoli in 1152. Raymond holds the distinction of being the first recorded Latin to fall victim to the Order of Assassins. As they rode into Tripoli, Raymond and two companions were attacked by a squad of Assassins who pulled the three men from their horses and stabbed them to death. Most believed Nur ed-Din had paid his one enemy, the Assassins, to kill his other enemy, Raymond, since Nur ed-Din quickly took advantage of Raymond's death by beginning raids around Tripoli. However, there were also rumors that Raymond's uncle, Baldwin III of Antioch, had ordered the assassination in order to settle a family succession dispute. In April 1192, Conrad of Montferrat, Lord of Tyre, King-elect of Jerusalem, was slain by two Assassins who had feigned conversion to Christianity in order to get close to him. One Assassin stabbed Montferrat and was captured. The second escaped the scene, only to attack Montferrat a second time in the church where Montferrat had been taken for treatment of his wounds. The first theory was that an angered Assassin grand master had ordered Montferrat killed in retaliation for Conrad having pirated a ship carrying Assassin property. However, under torture, the captured Assassin claimed Richard the Lionhearted ed had paid for Conrad's murder. As a matter of fact, a week after Conrad's assassination, Count Henry of Champagne, Richard's nephew, did became King of Jerusalem.

• • • • •

Over the years, the Order of Assassins had, at one time or another, made pacts and treaties with (or at least had been accused of making pacts with) rival Muslims, opportunistic crusaders, and godless Mongols. But despite a reputation for treachery and amorality when it came to choosing strange bedfellows, the Assassin sect was no more whorish than all the other opportunists and special interest groups making and breaking alliances and treaties on a daily basis, as fit their self-interest or the needs of survival. During the Middle Ages, it was not surprising to find Christians allied with Muslims against fellow Christians and brother Muslim betraying brother Muslim. A few examples:

- 1129: Assassins conspired with Baldwin to betray Damascus.
- 1149: Assassins allied with Prince Raymond of Antioch against Nur ed-Din.
- 1152: Baldwin II of Antioch conspired with Assassins to murder Raymond of Antioch (?).
- 1174: Aleppine Assassins and King of Jerusalem signed treaty against Nur ed-Din (and Templars).
- 1174: Assassins hired by Saladin to poison Nur ed-Din (?).
- 1183: Aleppine Assassins openly allied with Saladin.
- 1192: Richard the Lionhearted signed separate peace treaty with Saladin.
- 1194: King Henry of Jerusalem allied with Assassin sect.
- 1213: Pope refused to investigate allegations the Knights Hospitallers have allied with Assassins.
- 1221: Assassin leader Grand Master Muhammad II converted traditionally Shiite Assassin sect to the Sunnite branch of Islam. Muhammad died shortly thereafter, believed murdered by Assassin Shiite purists.
- 1227: Assassins signed peace treaty with Shah of Khourazmn against encroaching Mongols.
- 1228: Assassins "allied" with Mongols after treaty with Shah of Khourazmn collapsed.
- 1228: Frederick II, Holy Roman Emperor, king of Sicily and leader of the Sixth Crusade, sends tribute to the grand master at Alamut. Planning to assert his claim to Jerusalem, Frederick can not afford to have the Assassins at his back.
- 1231: Assassins implicated in murder of Shah of Khourazmn.
- 1238: Assassin envoys visited courts of England and France to propose alliance against Mongols.
- 1251: Assassins killed Mongol leader Jagatai.
- 1261: Following the ill-fated Seventh Crusade, in an extraordinary summit, Louis IX of France, grand masters of both the

Templars and the Hospitallers, and envoys from the Assassin grand master met. The true agenda discussed at this meeting has been the subject of endless speculation by conspiracy theorists. One version has envoys from the Assassin sect giving Louis a choice: the king of France must pay the Assassin sect tribute or issue an order barring the Templars and Hospitallers from extorting tribute from Assassin sect families living in their territory. Another version has the meeting laying the foundations for the rise of freemasonry and the international shadow cabal known as the Illuminati. More on these speculations in the next section.

THE FALL OF THE HOUSE OF HASAN

In January 1166, Hasan the Mad, grand master of the Alamut Assassins, was stabbed to death by his brother-in-law whom he had angered by changing Shiite-Islamic law and by proposing an alliance with the hated Sunnite Seljuks. Ironically, Hasan the Mad's bloodline continued with his son, Muhammad II, ruling as grand master from 1166 to 1210. Muhammad II continued his mad father's "resurrectionism" revival by declaring that the word of the living Imam himself was above that of dead prophets.

Muhammad II was succeeded by his son, Hasan III, during whose reign (1210-1221) the Mongols invaded Persia. Desperate for an alliance to save the Order, Muhammad II declared that the traditionally Shiite Assassin sect would convert en masse to the Sunnite branch of Islam! Whether this was a true conversion or merely a ploy to win needed Sunnite allies hardly matters, since Muhammad II died shortly afterward of dysentery (or poison) and was replaced by his 9-year-old son, Muhammad III. Also known as Aladdin, Muhammad III served as grand master from 1221 to 1255. Until Aladdin came of age, the order was ruled by a regent-vizier and the Red Circle, who purged all Sunni influence from the Assassin sect.

By 1222 Mongols were massacring their way west through Persia, slaughtering one million during the six-month siege of Herat. Bowing to pressure posed by the threat of fast-approaching Mongols, in 1227 Aladdin signed a peace treaty with the Shah of the Kingdom of Khourazmn, agreeing to pay the Shah tribute in exchange for an alliance against the advancing Mongols. However, when the Shah discovered that Assassins had infiltrated his bodyguard, staff, and his military, he ordered the infiltrators burned alive and began openly persecuting the Assassin sect. In retaliation against the Shah, and in an effort to ingratiate themselves with the invaders, Aladdin's agents began supplying strategic intelligence to the advancing Mongols.

Aladdin's plan was a classic: get a dog to eat a dog, i.e., get the Mongols—a looming threat—to destroy the immediate threat posed by the rampaging Shah. Unfortunately, after the Khourazmn Shah was murdered in 1231, the Khourazmn kingdom ceased to exist and the Mongols no longer needed the Assassins' intelligence. As a result, Mongol tolerance for the potentially troublesome assassins waned. Proposing a formal alliance between his sect and the Mongols, Grand Master Aladdin sent envoys to the Mongol capital in Karakorum, but the envoys were refused an audience because it was feared they plotted murder. Insulted by the snub, Aladdin struck back, killing Mongol leader Jagatai in 1251. Enraged by the murder of his brother, in 1252 Mongol leader Hulagu invaded the Alamut region and besieged Castle Alamut, intent on wiping out the whole of the assassin sect. Playing for time, Aladdin's successor Rukn ad-Din Khurshah, grand master from 1256 to 1276, petitioned the Mongols for peace. Hulagu refused and ordered Khurshah to destroy all Assassin strongholds and submit himself to Mongol justice. There is evidence Khurshah started doing as ordered as a ploy, all the while making plans to go underground.

In November of 1256, Khurshah and his entourage submitted to Hulagu after being guaranteed safe passage to the Mongol capitol. A month later, Castle Alamut fell and was leveled by the Mongols. Other Assassin strongholds continued to hold out. The last, Girdkuh, finally fell in 1257. Of no further use to the Mongols, Khurshah and his entourage were reportedly ambushed and slaughtered by Mongols, marking the end of the Persian-Alamutine Assassins.

In the next section we examine evidence that the Persian Assassins did not completely succumb to the Mongols, that Khurshah was not killed but rather he and members of the elite Red Circle escaped.

STONE KILLERS

After destroying Alamut, Mongol forces marched west into

Syria. By the close of 1258, Hulagu took Baghdad and Aleppo, where he massacred all Muslims but spared the Christians. In March of 1260, Hulagu's general, Kitboga, a Nestorian Christian, took Damascus. Having conquered Persia and Syria, Hulagu turned his attention south toward Egypt. He sent envoys to the Mameluke sultan in Cairo, demanding submission to the Mongol empire. The Mamelukes gave the Mongols a taste of their own medicine by killing the envoys. (Ten years earlier, the Egyptian's Mameluke warrior-slaves had staged a coup overthrowing their Egyptian masters. The Mamelukes had no intention of submitting themselves to another master.)

Preferring to fight Mongols in Palestine rather than Egypt, Mameluke forces invaded north into Palestine. In a decisive battle in 1260, Mameluke and Mongol armies clashed at the Battle of Goliath's Springs near Nazareth. When the dust settled, the invincible Mongols were in retreat.

After defeating the Mongols at Goliath's Springs, the victorious Egyptian sultan had his eye on returning to Cairo, but his most trusted and able general, the Mameluke Rukn ad-Din Baibars, architect of the Mongol defeat, had his eye on the empire. In October 1260, Rukn ("stone") Baibars stabbed the sultan in the back (literally) and seized the Egyptian throne.

Still flushed from victory over the Mongols, his fellow Mamelukes rallied behind Baibars' banner. By 1268 they had conquered Syria, taking first Damascus, then Antioch, and finally Aleppo, center of the Syrian Assassins. Most Assassin leaders had actively fought against the Mongols, but a few Assassin castle masters had surrendered their strongholds to the advancing horde.

As Baibars consolidated his power in Syria, Assassin lands and castles recaptured from retreating Mongols were returned to the sect, but those castle masters who had surrendered to the Mongols were executed. Baibars then ordered that tribute from Assassins formally going to Knights Hospitallers be given to the Mamelukes. Baibars also cut in half the tribute to be paid. These actions made Baibars very popular in Assassin circles, as was his intention. Unlike Hulagu, Baibars had no plans for either exterminating the Assassin sect or living in fear of their poisoned blades. Instead, Baibars planned to employ the Assassins to do what they did best: spy on his opponents and exterminate his enemies.

Better the blood of one than the blood of many when it comes to settling a dispute. Like any able commander, Baibars preferred the economy of deciding a dispute with the death of a single enemy rather than the deaths of thousands on both sides in a protracted war. For example, on August 17, 1270, an Aleppine Assassin unleashed by Baibars targeted French crusade leader Philip of Montfort, Lord of Tyre. Trained to pass himself off as a Christian, the Assassin struck while Montfort and his son were kneeling in their cathedral. In June 1272, Prince Edward (soon King Edward I of England) was stabbed five times in Acre by an Assassin disguised as a Levantine Latin pretending to be a Christian. Stabbed with a poisoned blade, Edward was stricken for weeks but survived. The Assassin had gotten close to Edward by bringing gifts to the prince's wife. Although Baibars had signed a peace treaty with Edward, many thought Baibars and the Mameluke governor of Ramleh were behind the plot.

Better the plume than poniard (a poniard is a dagger), i.e., better ink than blood. Though born and bred a warrior, Baibars had buried enough friends and comrades to prefer making alliances and treaties rather than having to watch men die on the battlefield. When the Knights Hospitallers, who resented Baibars seizing the tribute they had previously squeezed from Assassin supporters, openly defied Baibars, he decided to teach them a lesson, but didn't want to have to fight the Knights Templars as well. As a result, in 1271 Baibars made a secret deal with the Knights Templars via Assassin contacts whereby the Templars would voluntarily abandon their Castle Blanc at Safita, thus opening the way for Baibars' unrestricted assault on nearby Krak des Chevaliers, the Knights Hospitallers' castle-fortress.

In addition to preventing the needless loss of Templars blood, the destruction of their rivals' castle also suited the Templars' agenda. Baibars subsequently attacked Krak des Chevaliers with a large force including a contingent of Syrian Assassin sappers. Any Hospitallers captured were beheaded in full view of the castle's defenders. After 10 days of bombardment and undermining by Assassin sappers, the castle fell. By 1273 Baibars occupied all the Assassins' castles, had final approval over the appointment of their officers, and was de facto grand master of the Order.

In 1275, assassins with Baibars' blessing recaptured Alamut, only to lose it a year later. Ironically, Baibars himself was killed by poison he intended for a rival prince whom he had invited to a banquet on July 1, 1277. Somehow the cups were accidentally (?) switched, and Baibars died the agonizing death he had intended for his guest. Baibars' Mameluke successors continued effectively employing Baibars' stone killers to spy on potential opponents and kill enemies until the Mameluke dynasty was defeated by the Ottomans in 1517.

In 1238 envoys from the grand master of the Order of Assassins visited the courts of both England and France to urge an alliance of Christians and Muslims against the Mongols, but the Assassins' call for a Euro-Islamic alliance fell on deaf ears. In fact, it was the Europeans' grand hope that Mongols and Muslims would kill each other off. Then, after both sides had exhausted themselves, the Europeans would move into the Middle East and pick up the pieces. Disappointed, the Assassin whom the envoys had left with the European kings had a final cryptic prediction from the grand master: "The same serpent that feasts in *my* garden today will tomorrow draw it's succor from *your* heart." The Europeans laughed, thinking the grand master's riddle referred to the advancing Mongol horde.

It didn't.

CHAPTER FOUR

The Evolution of the Assassins: From Freebooters and Freemasons to Modern-Day Terrorists

"He who fights with monsters, let him be careful lest he thereby become a monster."

—Nietzsche

At this point the reader should have a solid grasp of the history of the Order of Assassins up until the time the Mongols were defeated. The reader should also have a good idea of how treacherous the Assassins were, how they would spend years lying in wait to strike if that was necessary, and how committed Assassins were to their masters and their craft. In this chapter we will simply note the most important and interesting of events from the 12th century up until 1996, with commentary on especially critical events and people.

IMPORTANT DATES, FACTS, AND EVENTS

1147 to 1270
European infighting largely hamstrings many nations' and factions' ability to crush the Order of Assassins in a kind of early Cold War.

1180s
Sicilian authorities wage war against the Avengers, a Sicilian secret society specializing in nocturnal assassinations.

1184

English knight Robert of St. Albans defects from the Templars and becomes a Muslim. He later leads an army for Saladin against the French in Jerusalem.

1186

Avenger grand master is hung; Order of Avengers believed wiped out. However, many believe that the Aleppine Assassins were an offshoot of the Avengers. Secret societies such as the Beati Paoli and the Black Hand can be traced to the Avengers. The Black Hand would later be known as the Mafia.

1213

The Templars take the side of King Bohemond against the Hospitallers after the Hospitallers are implicated in the murder of Bohemond's son and the patriach of Jerusalem.

1261

King Louis IX of France convenes a meeting of the leaders of the northern consortium in Acre, with the grand masters of both the Order of Assassins and Knights Templars in attendance. Louis proposes that they join him and six powerful merchant groups—to be collectively known as the *illuminati* or enlightened ones—in a scheme to control Europe, the Middle East, Far East, and Africa rather than fight each other for control. The Assassin grand master accepts, but the Templars grand master refuses.

1271

The Hospitallers lose their main castle in the Holy Land (Krak des Chevalliers) after the Templars reportedly make a deal with Mameluke warlord Baibars.

1305

King Philip IV of France seizes Pope Boniface VIII and installs a puppet pope, Clement V. Popes remain under direct French control until 1377, the period becoming known as the Babylonian Captivity.

12 September 1307

Royal officers throughout France receive two sealed letters from King Philip. The first instructs the recipients to prepare their troops for action (against the Templars) and tells them not to open the second until the evening of 12 October. By the morning of 13 October, nearly every Templars in France is in custody. Edward II of England (Philip's son-in-law) likewise seizes what he believes to be all the Templars in England, Wales, Ireland, and Scotland. However, Robert the Bruce, King of Scotland, defies Edward's order and secretly establishes the Order of H.R.M./Knights R.S.Y.C.S. from the Templars in his service.

1311
With the issuance of a papal decree, the Knights Templars officially ceases to exist after four years of persecution. Grand Master

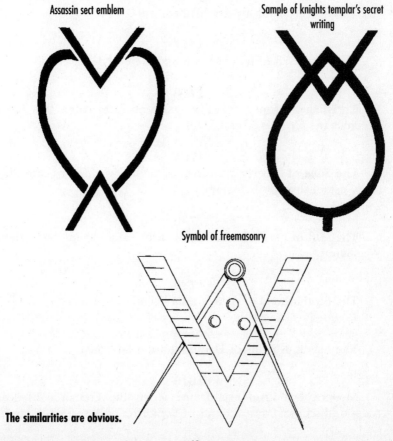

Assassin sect emblem

Sample of knights templar's secret writing

Symbol of freemasonry

The similarities are obvious.

De Molay and his lieutenant, Guy of Auvegne, are burned at the stake, still proclaiming their innocence.

1314

King Robert the Bruce ("Robert Bruce") defeats King Edward II at Bannock, thus securing Scottish independence until the 18th century. King Robert, in recognition of the commoners who fought for his cause, allows guilds of working men—Freemasons—to join the new Order. This revised Order became known as the Brotherhood of True Scots Rite Masonry, which would eventually spread to other countries and faiths under the generic name Freemasonry; eventually six million members would be claimed worldwide.

1624

The Rosecrucians are established.

1717

The first Scots Rite Lodge is founded in England.

1760

Christian masonry takes its current form after the Bible becomes the Order's "Great Light."

1765

The Sons of Liberty, an offshoot of the Freemasons, are officially established in the colonies.

1776

The Illuminati of Germany are established by Adam Weishaupt.

1780

The Brotherhood of Asia is established in Germany.

1781

The Asiatic Knights of Hamburg are established.

1810

Modern Ismailism established when the French consul at Aleppo "discovers" descendants of the Order of Assassins living in

Persia; the consul recognizes as their leader a man claiming to be a direct descendant of the fourth Assassin grand master, Hasan II.

1836

The first Muslims are accepted into the Brotherhood.

1865

The first Jews and Hindus are accepted into the Brotherhood.

1928

The Muslim Brotherhood is established; it would become the foundation of all modern Islamic terrorist groups.

1931

Elijah Muhammad founds the Temple of Islam in Detroit; many suspect he was an initiate of Prince Hall Masonry and the Moorish Science Temple (African-American offshoots of Scots Rites Masonry).

1946

Jewish terrorists use the Assassin tactic of mass killings by blowing up the King David Hotel, killing 91. They also slaughter 254 Palestinian civilians in the village of Deir Yassin.

1952

Anwar Sadat suspected of being involved in the overthrow of King Farouk by Muslim Brotherhood.

1954

Muslim Brotherhood banned in Egypt.

1956

Muslim Brotherhood begins *fedayeen* attacks into Israel.

1965

Malcom X, heir-apparent to Elijah Muhammad, is assassinated by a Black Muslim hit team.

1971

Palestinian/Arabic terror period begins with the unleashing

of the Palestine Liberation Organization's (PLO) mad dog, Black September.

1972
Black September terrorists massacre Israeli olympic team in Munich.

1975
Elijah Muhammad dies; Black Muslims split into two factions, with the Reverend Louis Farrakhan leading the radical Nation of Islam.

1977
Twelve *Hanafi* Black Muslim members seize three buildings in Washington, DC, killing one and taking 134 hostage.

1981
Egyptian President Anwar Sadat assassinated; Muslim Brotherhood believed behind the assassination.

Early 1980s
FBI discovers Libyan agents are funneling large sums of money into a Chicago-based pseudo-Islamic group known as *El Rukn* ("The Stone").

18 October 1983
U.S. Embassy in Beirut destroyed by suicide car-bomber; 50 killed.

23 October 1983
U.S. Marine Amphibious Unit barracks destroyed by suicide truck bomber; 241 killed.

1995
June: Egyptian President Hosni Mubarak survives assassination attempt by Muslim Brotherhood. August: More than 300 members of Muslim Brotherhood arrested by Egyptian security forces.

1996
Sheik Omar Abdel-Rahman—a Muslim cleric—and nine members of his Queens-based terrorist organization are convicted of the

World Trade Center bombing, which killed six and injured more than 1,000. (Had the plot succeeded as planned, tens of thousands would have been killed.)

PART TWO

CHAPTER FIVE

Fist and Fire

"All warfare is based on deception."

—Sun Tzu,
The Art of War

"Allah's Messenger named War: Deceit."

—Abu Huraira,
Shihih Al-Bukhari

THE RULES OF WAR

Every major military since the dawn of warfare tens of thousands of years ago has fashioned certain rules or principles to better achieve victory. Islamic forces were no different.

Islamic Warfare Rules

It is a rule of war that no battle plan survives first contact with the enemy. In other words, your enemy determines your strategy. In war you adapt or die, period. In keeping with this idiom, Arabic warfare strategy changed after the advent of Islam, and changed again with the coming of the Crusades.

Pre-Islamic Warfare

Prior to the coming of Muhammad, internecine warring

between Arab tribes was the norm. This infighting in many ways resembled the type of warring common between Native American tribes: raiding aimed at seizing goods, slaves, and brides rather than at seizing territory. When serious conflicts took place between Arab tribes, it was generally over vital oasis watering rights, or over real or imagined insults. Pre-Islamic Arab warriors possessed a warrior ethic and etiquette centered around a code of honor comparable to the Bushido of the Japanese samurai. This Arabic warrior code was comprised of two concepts: *islam* and *ghira*. In pre-Muhammad Arabic culture, the concept of "islam" referred to an attribute of manliness, combining virility and virtue, and was often applied to a warrior exhibiting special heroics in battle.

Inherent in the concept of islam was a devil-may-care attitude toward death and an acceptance ("submission to") the dictates of *qismah*, "duty or destiny." In English, *qismah* is often rendered *kismet*, a synonym for "fate." Only after the sixth century coming of the prophet Muhammad did the meaning of the word *islam* take on the more specific religious meaning of "submission" to Allah, the god of Muhammad.

The second major motivating concept for pre-Islamic Arabic warriors was *ghira*. Ghira ("respect") is in many ways similar to the Asian concept of *face*. A warrior failing to defend his honor or avenge a wrong against his person or his tribe was considered lacking in ghira. An affront to ghira required that reparation be paid, often in blood. Predictably, real or imagined affronts to ghira led to long-standing blood feuds. Slights between individuals often escalated to involve whole tribes. Of course, like the chivalry of the Christian Knights or the Bushido Code of the Samurai, the Arabic warriors' adherence to the ideals of islam and ghira often fell short. Despite these ideals, Arab warriors were not above resorting to guile and treachery to accomplish their aims: "To sneak up behind someone and slit his throat from ear to ear was viewed [by pre-Muhammad Arabs] as the right thing to do in certain situations, and the person who did it was viewed as a hero." (Robert Morey, *The Islamic Invasion: Confronting the World's Fastest Growing Religion*.)

Muhammad and War

"Verily Allah has enjoined goodness to everything; so when you kill, kill in a good way and when you slaughter, slaughter in a good way. So every one of you should sharpen his knife and let the slaughtered animal die comfortably."

—The Prophet Muhammad,
Al-Jami-us-Sahih, DCCXCV

Despite all-too-common Western depictions of Muhammad as a wild-eyed, bloodthirsty desert demon, he was, in fact, a man who preferred diplomacy to destruction, talking to taking heads. Yet when the time came to take scimitar in hand, Muhammad held no illusions about the nature of warfare. Some scholars translate Muhammad's summation of war as "war is stratagem." In any case, the meaning and intent is clear.

It is intriguing that Muhammad's succinct summation of the nature of war so closely resembles that used by renowned Chinese warrior Sun Tzu, who summed up the essence of war in his *Ping Fa (The Art of War)*. Written during China's tumultuous Warring States Period (453-221 B.C.E.), *The Art of War* remains to this day unrivaled in its discussion of war strategy and is still widely regarded today not just as a military treatise, but as a guide to such diverse subjects as philosophy and finances. *The Art of War* was already 1,000 years old by the time Muhammad began his religious crusade. Did Muhammad read, or was he otherwise exposed to, the strategy of Sun Tzu? Recall that before embarking on his religious crusade, Muhammad ran a caravan business, a vocation that brought him into contact with tales and travelers from many lands. At the very least, Muhammad could have picked up snippets of strategy while sitting around caravan campfires or while conversing with travelers, merchants, mendicants, and mercenaries from the Far East.

On the other hand, Muhammad's summation of war might simply be insight on his part. Perhaps good strategy is simply common sense which, unlike ignorance, is not all that common. Interestingly enough, there is a saying attributed to Muhammad that perhaps provides a clue: "Seek science, even in China."

• • • • •

According to *Hadith* (the recorded sayings and actions of Muhammad), the prophet forbade Muslims from fighting one another:

"When two Muslims fight each other with their swords, both the murderer as well as the murdered will go to the Hell-fire."

In preparing his followers for the battles he knew would surely come, Muhammad taught his followers that they should not desire an encounter with the enemy, but that it was essential to show "firmness" during such an encounter. According to noted author Eddie Stone in his *Khomeini, the Shah, the Ayatollah, the Shi'ite Explosion*, Muhammad set humane standards of warfare which his followers were commanded to observe:

- All agreements and treaties were to be honored.
- Treachery was to be avoided.
- Wounded enemies were not to be mutilated.
- Enemy dead were not to be disfigured.
- Women and children were not to be slain.
- Properties such as crops and orchards, as well as sacred objects, should be spared from destruction.

Allah's messenger indeed disapproved of the killing of women and children. We are left to wonder then what the prophet of Islam would have thought of the intentional bombing of a bus packed full of women and children?

Far from having his head in the clouds, Muhammad's war strategy was realistic as noted by his instructions in the Quran:

Then, when the sacred months have passed, slay the idolators wherever ye find them, and take them captive, and beseige them, and prepare for them each ambush. But if they repent and establish worship and pay the poor-due, then leave their way free. Lo! Allah is forgiving, merciful.

As this passage indicates, Muhammad understood the dynamics of taking prisoners (possible converts, individuals who could be ransomed, enslaved); the necessity of the seige; and the usefulness of catching an enemy napping. He understood the practicality of ambush in a guerrilla campaign. In Arabic, the word often used for ambush, *an-najash* ("drawing out") refers to a ploy of bidding high to trick another bidder into bidding higher and eventually overbidding. Narrator Al-Jami-us-Sahih relates the story of an ambush by Mohammad upon the Banu Mustliq tribe ". . .while they were unaware and their cattle were having a drink at the water." According to this account, Muhammad's forces killed those who resisted and enslaved others.

Jihad and Martyrdom

"A man asked Muhammad, 'What is the best deed?' Muhammad replied, 'To believe in Allah and his Messenger.' The man then asked, 'What is the next in goodness?' The Prophet replied, 'To participate in Jihad in Allah's cause.'" (Abu Huraira, Shihih Al-Bukhari.)

No other Islamic concept has been more misunderstood by Westerners, and more manipulated by self-serving Middle Eastern power-mongers, than the concept of Jihad (Holy War). Jihad grew out of the Arabic ghira blood-feud mentality that required all trespass against honor to be met, all slights avenged. Before Muhammad, jihad was applied generically to mean any combat or campaign undertaken to assuage ghira. Under Muhammad, Jihad was applied specifically to crusades undertaken for the purpose of advancing or defending Islam. Raiding between rival Arabic tribes for revenge or slaves was a way of life before Muhammad. Under Muhammad, raiding was elevated to a religious duty and eventually expanded beyond Arabia. While booty could still be taken, Muhammad made plain that the underlying justification for raiding and conquest was spreading the word of Allah:

A man came to Muhammad and asked, 'One man fights for war booty; a second fights for fame and a third fights to show off; which of them fights in Allah's cause?' Muhammad replied, 'He who fights that Allah's Word triumphs, that man fights in Allah's cause.' (Abu Huraira, Shihah Al-Bukhari.)

Pre-Islamic Arabic warriors believed paradise awaited any warrior who died bravely in battle. To this traditional belief, Muhammad added an extra element of religious fervor and reward: In Islam, any Muslim dying in Jihad was a martyr and earned his place in Paradise:

A man asked Muhammad to show him a deed equal to

Jihad in reward. Muhammad told the man, 'I do not find such a deed.' (Abu Huraira, Shihah Al-Bukhari.)

According to Islamic tradition, a Muslim dying in Jihad has all his sins blotted out and automatically wins an honored place in heaven, the garden of paradise. In addition, a martyr:

- receives a crown embedded with an invaluable ruby set in the center (an obvious symbolic reference to the halo and the acquisition of the mystic's "third eye" of enlightenment)
- is married to 72 dark-eyed celestial virgins
- and, perhaps most importantly, Allah intercedes for 70 of the martyr's relatives

• • • • •

Islam is not the only culture to promise its warriors reward in the next world if they but give up their lives in this one. The Norsemen believed that the warrior's paradise of Valhalla was the destiny of any Viking *berserker* or *wolfshirt* who died with sword in hand. Later, Christian knights were likewise promised heavenly reward if they died during a "holy" crusade. Assassin sect members had even more reason to embrace martyrdom in the sect's service, since, as recruits, they had already been given a foretaste of "paradise" in Hasan's magical garden.

Jihad has been manipulated down to the present day as an excuse for Islamic crusade and conquest. Today, terrorists throughout the Middle East and the world use Jihad as a call for the creation of a one-world, trans-Islamic empire. However, moderate Islamic scholars dispute that Muhammad's original call for Jihad was meant as a perpetual cry for constant war:

Actually the Koran's call to arms, or Jihad ("holy war"), relates to a specific episode when the Prophet prepared to attack his enemies from the city of Mecca. It was never intended as a prescription for permanent warfare against the rest of the world. (Sai'd Al-Ashmawy, Islam's Real Agenda.)

These moderates go on to point out that suicidal actions,

such as suicide bombings, are expressly forbidden to devout Muslims: "Allah said: My slave has caused death on himself hurriedly, so I forbid Paradise to him." (Abu Huraira, Shihih Al-Bukhari.)

Perhaps someone should inform such fanatical groups as Hamas and Hizbullah about this.

ASSASSIN RULES OF WARFARE

The only rule to the Order of Assassins' strategy for war was: There are no rules!

Assassin indoctrination led recruits step-by-step through a transcendence of moral qualms and restraints toward a mind-set that allowed Assassin agents to act without hesitation. The dagger's duty is not to ponder, but merely to remain firm when plunged forward.

Religious fanatics and psychopaths share one thing in common: the belief that the end justifies the means.

Al Jebr

The Assassins' overall fighting strategy, which included battle tactics, is known as Al Jebr ("calculation"). It is from this word that we get our English word for mathematical calculation, algebra.

Al Jebr consists of four steps.

Understanding Self

This is taking a realistic assessment of your strengths and weaknesses, honing both your mental and physical reflexes.

Understanding Others

Deciphering intent in others is what this is, i.e., discovering weaknesses that can be exploited.

Understanding Flux of Circumstance

Here the warrior is making a realistic assessment of situational factors such as time, place, and terrain.

Effective Execution

This is your understanding of the first three steps. Action without knowledge is foolishness. Knowledge without action is cowardice.

• • • • •

Danger increases with proximity. The closer an enemy can get to you, the more danger you are in. Consequently, the closer an Assassin could get to an enemy—literally getting inside an enemy's physical defenses or figuratively getting inside his mind—the easier the accomplishment of the Assassin's mission.

Intelligence, Strategy, and Execution

Al Jebr aims at penetrating ever deeper into an enemy's fortress or mind by employing three successive steps:

1. Intelligence gathering
2. Strategy development (based on intelligence gathered)
3. Execution of that strategy

These three steps require not only the deployment of physical factors (troops, traps, etc.), but also a studied consideration of psychological factors, both your enemy's and your own.

Psychological Warfare

Assassin grand masters used psychology to determine an enemy's intent as well as when and where an enemy was most vulnerable. Assassin psychological warfare considers two aspects: the psychology of self and the psychology of others. The more you know about yourself, the better prepared you will be to deal with others. Conversely, by uncovering the weaknesses of others—secret fears and obvious foibles—the better you become at perfecting and protecting yourself against such weaknesses. In other words, Al Jebr aims at the systematic penetration of an enemy's mind, circumventing impressive mental facades and defensive rationalization barriers to discover his secrets: Hidden fears and desires that can be manipulated to an Assassin's advantage.

An enemy's fear, greed, arrogance, and other weaknesses are exploited through the use of the nine-gates philosophy (discussed more fully in a moment). Defeating a foe using a psychological ploy is always preferable to having to kill him. Remember that Hasan ibn-Sabbah's preference was to try educating foes before having to assassinate them. Better a warning than a wounding.

• • • • •

When respected Sunnite scholar Razi began preaching against Ismaili doctrine, Grand Master Muhammad II sent an Assassin agent to dissuade Razi. Posing as a student for seven months, the agent finally succeeded in gaining Razi's confidence. One day, as Razi was preparing to make another sermon, the Assassin "student" put a dagger to Razi's throat and ordered him to stop preaching against Ismailis. Predictably, the wise scholar decided to temper his tongue. Asked later why he'd refrained from preaching against the Ismailis, Razi quipped: "The Assassins' arguments are too pointed!"

The Psychology of Self

Early on in their training, Assassin recruits were introduced to mental disciplines designed to steel them in the face of danger and death. Assassins aimed at cultivating a mind-set that allowed them to act with calculation but without hesitation. For an Assassin, hesitation equals death.

In order to acquire a level of training and awareness where thought and action were one, Assassin recruits were taught a variety of mental gymnastics akin to and perhaps derived from Indian yogic disciplines.

Two of the most useful of these Assassin mental practices were meditation and hypnosis.

Meditation

Meditation teaches the body patience when waiting is required and calms the mind when clear-headed calculation is called for. Assassin mental disciplines in general, and their meditation practices in particular, are known as Khilwat *weave*.

Arabian tales of "magic carpets" carrying adventurers aloft, to any clime or dimension, are actually thinly disguised references to Sufi (Muslim mystics) meditating on their prayer rugs. The magic carpet is also symbolic of the sacred robe Muhammad used to lift the "black stone" at the rebuilding of the Ka'ba.

Khilwat meditation is practiced by sitting with legs crossed in a comfortable position, back straight, head slightly bowed. The meditator's hands are held approximately three inches out from the chest at heart level with the fingers entwined to form one of four mystic "weaves."

Each Khilwat weave is associated with and designed to infuse the meditator with the particular attitude and power represented by that weave:

Earth weave = courage and strength
Water weave = morality and justice
Fire weave = reasoning and wisdom
Air weave = temperance and spirituality

Hypnosis and self-hypnosis were taught to recruits as methods for improving control over self and for manipulating others.

Self-hypnosis taught recruits how to relax physically and calm their mind in preparation for going on a mission. During meditation, recruits were given a key word, for example, "calm," which

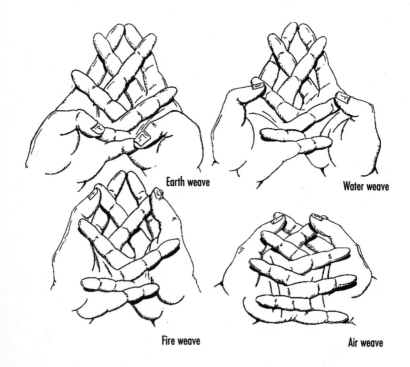

Earth weave

Water weave

Fire weave

Air weave

Illustration 3

they would chant when meditating. In stressful situations, by invoking this "key word" they had trained their body and mind to associate with relaxation, Assassins could "trick" their mind and body into relaxing. For combat training, recruits were taught a "trigger" word that they would shout (audibly or internally) each time they threw a punch or kick or thrust a weapon. Faced with a life-or-death situation, Assassins could then invoke this trigger word in order to ignite their flight/fight adrenaline response and release their power.

Hypnosis was also mastered by Assassins as a method of manipulating others. The same kind of hypnosis technique used by today's stage magicians to dazzle audiences were employed by Assassin grand masters with many sinister goals in mind. To induce or augment control over a hypnotized subject, Assassins often used a variety of drugs to make the subject more pliable. Hypnotized individuals could then be given post-hypnotic suggestions designed to be triggered when an Assassin agent whispered a specific trigger word in the subject's ear, or when the subject saw a trigger word in a written message. While the rule of thumb is that a hypnotized person cannot be made to do anything they wouldn't normally do, a post-hypnotic suggestion could be framed in such a way as to work to the Assassin's advantage.

For example, whereas a hypnotized servant would balk at the post-hypnotic suggestion, "You will kill your master while he sleeps," that same hypnotized servant would obey the post-hypnotic suggestion that, at a prescribed time, "You will open the locked window in your master's bedroom so that your master can enjoy the night breeze." The Assassin agent would then take advantage of that open window to do what he did best.

• • • • •

Sinan the Physician was a master at infiltrating agents into the courts and retinues of influential leaders. Visiting with these courts, Sinan would often exhibit his "powers" of mind control by instantly "hypnotizing" one of his host's guards. Sinan could then order this "hypnotized" guard to commit suicide or some other outrageous act, all to the shock and chagrin of the guard's master. Of course, the "hypnotized" guard was really one of Sinan's faithful agents who had infiltrated the court sometime before.

This same ploy is still used today by stage magicians and hypnotists who invite members from the audience up on stage to help them with an illusion. The audience member "picked at random" is really a confederate.

The Psychology of Others

Psychology and propaganda were used routinely within the Order of Assassins to inspire and otherwise manipulate followers. Young assassin recruits were eager to throw their lives away after tasting the forbidden fruit of paradise in the Old Man of the Mountain's magic garden of delights. Today's young Islamic fanatics are likewise all too eager to detonate the bomb strapped to their chest, having been promised paradise by their masters. This kind of psychological manipulation is not limited to Middle Eastern countries and culture.

Throughout history, religious figures and cult leaders have used superstition and the promise of paradise both to control followers and to galvanize them into throwing away their lives. As previously mentioned, the belief that the blood of Christ flowed through the veins of European royalty helped to keep Europe's feudal populace in line. For example:

- Trapped in a losing battle, 4th century emperor Constantine rallied his troops, winning the day and converting all of Rome to Christianity after claiming to have seen the "sign of the cross" hovering over the battlefield.
- At the mired seige of Antioch in 1098, the flagging morale of Christian crusaders was revitalized by the all-too-convenient discovery of the "holy lance," the spear believed to have been used to pierce the side of Christ.
- Muslim Caliph Omar, facing overwhelming odds, outfitted his troops in silken robes designed to reflect the dawning sun. To the opposing army, it appeared that there were angels among Omar's hosts.

In the Assassin bag of tricks, such ploys are known as *namima*, false information designed to create chaos and calamity. Namima covers ploys, propaganda, and deception of all sorts, from making the enemy think you have more troops than you do to feeding a list of phony contacts to compromised or otherwise unreliable agents. (An individual or agent dealing in namima is called a *qattat*.)

As an example of this, the Old Man of the Mountain needed to remove the loyal captain of a particular king's guard in order for an Assassin infiltrator, already planted in the king's guard, to move into the captain's position. Not wanting to arouse suspicion by simply murdering the captain, Hasan decided that a namima ploy was called for.

Discovering the captain's wife to be a regular patron of al ocal soothsayer, the Assassin grand master convinced (bribed or threatened) the ersatz psychic to give the captain's wife a special reading. The next time the woman visited the psychic, the psychic predicted that the woman's husband was going to divorce her. Distraught, she asked what she could do to prevent a divorce. As instructed by Hasan, the psychic gave the woman a "magic dagger" and told her that, on the night of the full moon, she must use the dagger to cut off a lock of her husband's hair while he slept. The wife was then to bring the lock of hair to the psychic, who promised to cast a spell designed to prevent the divorce.

Around the same time the psychic was telling the captain's wife to cut off a lock of her husband's hair, the captain received an anonymous warning that, on the night of the full moon, his wife planned to murder him! Predictably, come the night of the full moon, the captain, feigning sleep, sees his wife sneaking up on him, dagger in hand. Enraged, he kills his wife on the spot and is subsequently executed for her murder. And, as planned, the Assassin agent becomes the new captain of the guard.

The similarities between this true story and Shakespeares' *Othello* (written in 1604) are striking.

Whereas lying was universally despised in Arabic culture, namima disinformation was a vital weapon in the Assassin's arsenal.

The Nine Gates to the City

In calculating how to get close to an enemy, either to infiltrate or to assassinate, assassin trainees were taught that, like a great walled city, the mind and body of man has nine "gates" through which a knowledgeable Assassin might penetrate. An enemy's physical gates could be penetrated by physical techniques. Similarly, an enemy could also be attacked through his nine psychological gates via psychological attacks.

Physical gates included the eyes (two), ears (two), nose (two nostrils), mouth (one), urethra (one), and anus (one), totaling nine. Psychological gates consisted of sight, hearing, attraction, distraction, appetite, needs, sex, wants, and predictability, again totaling nine.

Physical Penetration

Assassin students were required to master the subject of human anatomy (what parts of the body were most susceptible to blows and dagger thrusts, how particular drugs and poisons worked) in preparation for physical assault.

- The eyes of an enemy can be attacked by blinding him with toxic liquids and powders. Eyes can be blinded by too much light as well and can be rendered almost useless with too little light.
- An enemy's ears can be startled by loud noises. A person's ears also control his balance; strong blows to the ears can shatter the ear drum, thereby unbalancing an opponent, producing pain, disorientation, and even death.
- Can't breath, can't fight. Mace and other toxics can interfere with an opponent's breathing (nose). Sharp blows to the nose can interfere with breathing and cause temporary blindness through tearing of the eyes. Strong punches to the midsection (diaphragm) can also interfere with breathing.
- Medieval assassins concocted special perfumes that, separate, were harmless, but when combined produced deadly gas.
- Anything a person eats (mouth) can be poisoned.
- The hands and fingers of an attacker can be counterattacked by stabs and cuts with sharp implements. Hands can also be crippled by blows from heavy objects and/or punches. Fingers can be broken through the use of grabbing or twisting breaks and locks.
- The wrist is the weak link connecting the hands ("guns") with the muscles ("ammunition") of the arm. Break this link and you make it impossible for an opponent to use his hands as weapons. The wrist can be dislocated by jerking an attacker's hand forward sharply. The wrist can also be incapacitated by heavy blows and/or tendon-severing cuts.
- The elbow can be jammed, taking power from a punch. The elbow can also be "locked out" and broken.

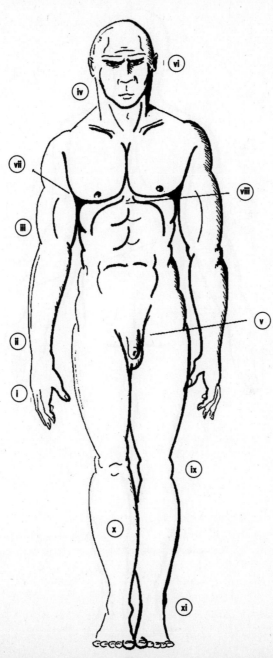

Illustration 4

71

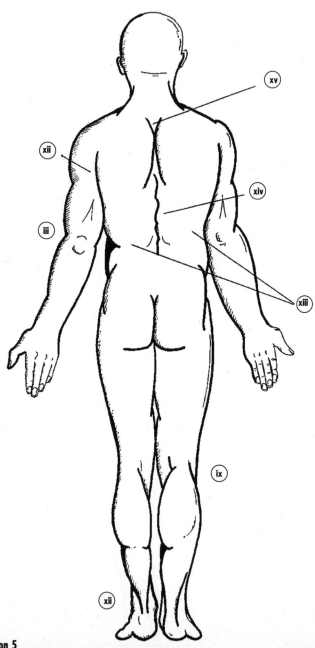

Illustration 5

- The neck and throat can be targeted with sharp implements and with hand blows during close-in fighting.
- The groin can be targeted with kicks, hand blows, and with stabbing implements, either from the front or the rear. The testicles and penis can be targeted with wrenching or squeezing grabs.
- The head can be targeted with hand strikes (when an opponent is standing) and foot blows (when an opponent is down), with heavy bludgeon blows, and with stabbing strikes.
- The armpit can be targeted any time an opponent raises his arm. Use a feigned overhead strike to make an opponent expose this vulnerable area. Attack into the armpit with clenching grabs where the pectoral (chest) muscle connects onto the upper arm. Stab into the armpit with stabbing implements and with stiff-finger strikes.
- The solar plexus can be attacked with punches, horizontal elbow blows, and with stabbing implements.
- The knee can be targeted with sweeping kicks and with stomps.
- The shin can be attacked with kicks and with painful downward scraping attacks.
- The foot and ankle can be attacked with stomps designed to impede strikes and with kicks designed to force an opponent off balance. The Achilles tendon at the back of the ankle can be attacked with debilitating stomps and with kicks again designed to throw your opponent off balance.
- The kidneys can be attacked with a variety of hand and foot blows, as well as with stabbing implements.
- The spine offers targets all along its length. The seventh vertebra is susceptible to forceful "hammer" blows from the fist and from bludgeons. This is also a major stabbing target when attacking from the rear.

Psychological Penetration

The nine-gates philosophy is also used to plot psychologically based attacks, such as when an enemy's eye and ear gates are tricked through the clever use of camouflage and disguise.

For example, after scouting the Persian fortress of al-Ubullah, Caliph Omar's lieutenant, Utbah, realized that a direct assault by his small force would be futile and decided instead to use a ruse. Utbah had the women in his camp sew extra flags, which he then hung on spears. These spears he gave to the women, ordering them to march behind his army, raising as much dust as possible. When the Persian defenders saw the Muslims advance and saw the amount of dust being raised, the defenders falsely assumed that Utbah's small force of 300 was merely the vanguard for a much larger army. The Persians quickly abandoned al-Ubullah, allowing Utbah to occupy the fortress and the surrounding countryside without firing a shot. This is an ancient ploy, one spoken of Sun Tzu's *The Art of War:* "In night fighting use many torches and drums, in day fighting many banners and flags in order to influence the sight and hearing of the enemy."

During World War II, Allied forces created phony airfields and army bases replete with straw soldiers, wooden planes, and inflatable trucks and tanks, all designed to fool the eye gates of Axis spies.

The ear gates can also be attacked through rumor and disinformation (namima). During the War of 1812, two young girls, alone at Scituate Light, Massachusetts, frightened away a British invasion force simply by playing a fife and drum up and down the shore, tricking the British into believing colonial troops were massing to defend against any landing.

Mouth gate ploys attack enemyies through their appetites and needs. We all must eat, making each of us susceptible to poisoning on a physical level. However, we can also be "poisoned" on a mental level.

"Appetite" also applies broadly to greed and to those things we think—or can be convinced—we need. Implanting "false" needs into a person's head is a tried and true ploy; just ask the master manipulators on Madison Avenue.

Metaphorically speaking, to use a nose gate ploy to trap a foe, we must first find something that either attracts him greatly or repels him greatly and then use that strong like or dislike to "lead him around by the nose." Psychologically, the nose gate is influenced by attraction and confused by distraction. Confidence schemers enter the lives of their victims through this unguarded gate. A sweet smell (a too-good-to-be-true deal, for example) catches a person's attention in the same way the smell of blood attracts a predatory animal.

In employing urethra gate manipulation, an enemy's desires and lusts are used against him. At the simplest level, a foe might be distracted and set up for murder by a damsel in distress (or young man, depending on the target's particular proclivity). At a deeper level, an enemy official might spy against his own government if you convince him that his talents would be more appreciated and respected by your side.

Anus gate strategy teaches us that we are all creatures of habit. Fearing the strange, we fall to the familiar. We take the same route home every day, eat at the same restaurant each weekend, and sooner or later we must all heed the call of nature. Around any one of these corners we turn on the way to these familiar spots, death can be waiting. Many a Muslim (Shiite founder Ali, for example) has been slain while attending mandatory prayers. The bottom line: human beings are predictable.

The Art of Espionage

In any time and clime, the goal of espionage is twofold: decipher the enemy's intent and mask your own. Knowledge is power, and intelligence, both the inherited kind and the gathered variety, is a coveted commodity, vital to the success of a mission and vital to the survival of an agent.

No one knows when or where the organized use of spies began. However, 2,500 years ago, Sun Tzu thought the use of spies so vital to strategy that he devoted an entire chapter in *The Art of War* to the subject.

Naturally, spies are nothing new in the Middle East. In the 13th century, the Hebrew warlord Joshua sent spies into the land of Canaan prior to his Israelite invasion. The prophet Muhammad also understood the need for spies, as it is recorded that the "reconnoiterer" Az-Zubair brought Muhammad vital information prior to the strategic Battle of Al-Ahzab. Assassin trainees were drilled in a regimen of espionage skills that would have made James Bond envious. This course of study included studying customs and religion, language, codes, disguise, infiltration, and escape and evasion. Recruits showing aptitude in certain areas were then given advanced espionage training.

Types of Spies

Assassin grand masters employed four types of agents.

Gatherers: These were persons living in a specific area who passed on bits of information, often without knowing that the information would eventually find its way to the Assassin grand master. Each piece of information might be unimportant in and of itself, but when put together with other fragments of information, emerging patterns were often revealed.

Turned Agents: Turned agents were also indigenous personnel (natives, officials, and sometimes captured enemy spies) who were convinced (through bribery, threats, or blackmail) to work for the Assassin cause.

False Agents: False agents were expendable. These agents were sent on impossible missions guaranteed to result in their death or capture. These agents were expected to fail and would be supplied with false information that would either be found on their bodies or tortured out of them. Such disinformation would consist of Assassin contacts (actually loyal courtiers) or false travel plans for individuals or caravans (designed to entice the readers into an ambush).

True Agents: These agents were of two types: sappers sent out on specific missions (attacks on castles, assassinations, ambushes) and sleepers, who were infiltrators and deep-cover agents.

Here's a tale of two sappers: In 1970, two hijackers commandeered a plane on a flight out of Teheran and forced it to fly to Baghdad, where they declared their intention to join General Taymor Bakhitiar's fight against the Shah of Iran. Bakhitiar welcomed these defectors with open arms. (In 1956, Bakhitiar had become the first chief of SAVAK, the Shah's dreaded secret police. By all reports, Bakhitiar took pleasure in personally torturing prisoners. His power grew in Iran until the Shah himself began to fear him. Finally, after being implicated in a 1967 plot to kill the Shah, Bakhitiar fled to Iraq.)

Three years later, a few days after the arrival of the two defecting hijackers, Bakhitiar and his two new friends embarked on a hunting expedition. The hunting was good for the two defectors. As soon as they saw their chance, they put a bullet through Bakhitiar's brain and fled back to Iran.

To this day, whether the two assassins were sent by the Shah himself or by the Iranian terrorist group Siahkal, whom Bakhitiar had ruthlessly suppressed, is not known.

If the plot used to assassinate Bakhitiar in 1970 sounds familiar, that's because it's the same plot Sinan the Physician used to kill Conrad of Montferrat in 1192. (See "The Art of Disguise" later in this chapter.)

As for sleeper agents, they are common in intelligence operations and are given sufficient funds and cover identities to allow them to insinuate their way into a particular clique, court, or community.

Positioned well in advance, sleepers give logistical help to other agents arriving later and use their established, trusted position to get close to notables, cutting them down when the order comes from their "controller" (spy master). Sleeper agents can spend years worming their way into trusted positions within an enemy stronghold and then remain in place for years, waiting for the single command from their leader to strike.

To show the extremes to which Assassin agents will go to insinuate themselves into an advantageous position, Zengi, father of Nur ed-Din, was murdered by an Assassin sleeper agent posing as a eunuch. (We need not ask how this Assassin successfully passed himself off as a eunuch. Obviously the agent had been chosen for the mission because he was a cut above other agents!) Assassin grand masters went so far as to purchase young European slaves, raise them in Assassin doctrine, then send them out to spy among the Christians.

It has been alleged that, after the breakup of the Order of Assassins, these Assassin-trained European sleepers helped found several European secret societies and Freemasonry lodges.

• • • • •

Assassin sleepers were skilled in all aspects of imposture and Assassin sappers were drilled in all manner of stealth in preparation for infiltration and in case they needed to escape or evade capture.

The Art of Stealth
The Assassin art of stealth, called *kasafat* ("eclipsed") included not only silent movement, but also the breaching of barriers (walls, moats, etc.). Assassin sappers slipping into crusader camps past guard dogs often did so naked, since it was believed that dogs never bark at a naked man. This also let sappers know that anyone they touched who was wearing clothes was the enemy. In modern

times, Arabs infiltrating French Foreign Legion posts in Algeria also used this ploy.

Before infiltrating a fortress, sappers oiled their bodies. This not only helped them to squeeze through small openings, but also allowed them to wiggle free if attacked.

The Art of Disguise

"The Jinn may take the form of animals like snakes, scorpions, camels, cows, goats, sheep, horses, mules, donkeys, and birds. They may also assume the form of humans. . ."

—Ibn Taymeeyah,
Essay on the Jinn

Called *taqiyah*, the art of disguise can be as simple as turning a reversible jacket inside out and pulling a cap down over your head in order to lose yourself in a crowd. To a sleeper agent spending months or years creating a deep-cover story, insinuating yourself into a community, court, or clique in order to get close enough to kill the target meant nothing.

In 1192, two well-educated and wealthy Syrians, from all outward appearances the very image of Muslim nobility, settled in the city of Tyre. Expressing an interest in converting to Christianity, the two quickly made friends amongst the Christians, including the leader of Tyre, Conrad of Montferrat, next in line for King of Jerusalem. Convinced of the two's sincerity, Conrad himself sponsored the two Muslims' baptism as Christians.

Conrad was very proud of his part in the conversion of the two "godless" Muslims. As a result, the two converts soon became permanent fixtures in Conrad's court and were often seen in his company.

Months passed. Then one day, Conrad was approached on the street by his two new friends. As Conrad heartily greeted them, one pinned Conrad's sword arm while the other repeatedly plunged a dagger deep into Conrad's body. The two "converts" were, of course, Assassin agents unleashed by Sinan the Physician, whom Conrad had angered by pirating a merchant ship carrying Assassin cargo.

• • • • •

The more things change, the more they stay the same. In November 1991, an assassin disguised as a journalist repeatedly stabbed the former king of Afghanistan in a failed assassination attempt.

CHAPTER SIX

Janna: Assassin Unarmed Combat

"So Moses struck him with his fist and killed him."

—The Quran

Before his untimely death in 1405, Mongol conqueror Tamerlane seemed undefeatable. In 1387, the warrior conquered Persia and by 1392 the Caucasus were under his control. In 1398 he invaded India and sacked Delhi. He then ran across Syria to defeat the Ottoman Turks in 1402.

Tamerlane's successes were in a great part due to his use of the nine blows military strategy. He divided his forces into three parts: a center and two wings. Each of these was composed of three divisions. During a battle, these nine divisions attacked in waves, delivering nine separate successive blows against enemy positions.

THE FOUNDATION OF JANNA

Assassin unarmed combat—*janna*—employs a strategy similar to Tamerlane's, relying on nine principle body weapons striking in a succession of blows designed to overwhelm an opponent.

Unarmed hand blows and blocks used in janna closely approximate those movements used when the hand is gripping a knife (or any other weapon for that matter). As with all reality-based martial arts, regardless of time or place, Assassin janna trainees were first required to master a course of hand-to-hand combat before progressing to armed combat forms. This common sense progression helped toughen trainees physically as well as psychologically, preparing them for violent one-on-one struggles. An initial course of unarmed combat study also helped instructors separate those students with natural fighting (and killing) ability from those requiring additional instruction and from those who would never be suited for what some modern-day assassins call "wet work." Effective mastery of unarmed combat provided Assassin operatives with an additional line of defense in the (unlikely) event they ever found themselves separated from their weapons.

THE NINE BLOWS OF JANNA

Assassin initiates learned the nine blows of janna during their training.

Hands
Janna hand blows primarily consist of three techniques: hammer-hand (closed-hand fist), knife-hand (palm blows and stiff-finger jabs), and the lion's paw (claw-hand/splayed fingers).

Hammer-Hand
Hammer-hand blows are performed exactly the same as blows delivered when gripping a knife or other stabbing weapon.

Knife-Hand
These strikes are extended-finger jabs mimicking the stabbing of a real knife blade into soft targets (eyes, the front of the throat, solar plexus). In addition, knife-hand/open-hand palm blows give the added advantage that once the palm blow makes contact, the hand can easily be closed and used for grabbing (jerking an opponent off balance, pulling him into another strike, etc.).

Lion's Paw
These clawing hands are also used to attack soft targets such as the eyes and throat.

Feet
Unlike most Far Eastern unarmed combat styles (karate, kung-

Illustration 6

fu), janna unarmed combat does not emphasize high kicking, concentrating instead on low-level kicks including covered-toe strikes forward and up (targeting the groin and bladder), sweeps and strikes with the instep, and heel stomps forward and down (designed to deliver the *coup de grace* to an opponent once he is knocked to the ground).

Elbows and Knees

These are used in janna as secondary, close-in weapons and as finishing-off weapons. An opponent's head can be pushed down to meet a rising knee. An elbow strike to the temple can kill an opponent.

The Head

Head butts and strikes can be employed in both offensive (the forward head butt) and defensive (the rear head butt when grabbed from behind) maneuvers.

• • • • •

It must be remembered that Assassin recruits were not trained to be unarmed fighters per se, but rather were trained to *kill* unarmed. It was vital that an assassin finish off a foe as quickly as possible, especially one encountered unexpectedly (such as when escaping from a castle). An Assassin sapper entering or exiting a castle had scant seconds to disable an unexpected sentry before an alarm could be sounded. As a result, janna emphasizes striking a foe with a single forceful blow designed to kill him, or at the very least knock him unconscious. Barring a single, decisive blow, assassins struck with a succession of three rapid blows designed to first stun and then kill a foe. Anything less would delay the assassin's ingress or egress.

When your escape depends on quick action, delay equals death.

UNARMED BLOCKING TECHNIQUES

Whenever possible, it is preferable to block any attack with a weapon in your hand. This applies whether your attacker is armed or unarmed. Any stout stick, rolled-up magazine, or similar weapon can be held flush with the forearm using the inside grip to augment blocking (see Illustration seven). It is especially important to protect the blocking/deflecting arm when defending against attack by a heavy bludgeon or blade.

Punches, kicks, and weapons blows can be effectively blocked or deflected with your arms.

Illustration 7

Rising Forearm Block

Similar to the rising forearm blocks of karate, the janna rising forearm block is designed to catch or deflect descending blows (unarmed or armed). This block can also be used to block a high kick aimed at your head. Your blocking forearm surface can be reinforced with a blade or stout stick held with the inside grip. Two rising forearm blocks crossed create an "X block."

Rising Half-Moon Block

Similar to the rising forearm block, the rising half-moon block travels in a half moon (semicircle) that allows it to first deflect an attack aimed at the head and then, by completing the half circle, trap the attacking arm before it can be withdrawn. The half moon sweeping arm block can be used with the blocking arm moving outwards from the body or to augment a turning inward block.

Cross-Body Block

This block is used to press an attacker's thrusting forward arm inwards toward his centerline, in effect knocking his body off balance. It is best utilized in conjunction with the angled avoidance stepping. The same basic movement employed in this block is used in an empty-hand palm-blow counterattack to an enemy's ribs or solar plexus. A solid fist strike (targeting an opponent's midsection) can be made using this same basic striking movement. However, blocking (or striking) with the open palm has the advantage of making it easier to seize the attacker's arm once it has been "shocked" by a forceful palm block or blow.

Descending Forearm Block

This powerful block is used to counter attacks (punches, kicks, knife) to your lower body and downward body blows aimed at your solar plexus. When countering kicks, use this same descending arm movement, targeting the attacker's extended leg with a hammer-hand strike.

Low-Level Half-Moon Block

Similar to the rising half-moon block, this block circles down and then up in a half circle. This block is ideal for deflecting and trapping an attacker's kicking leg.

Blocking-Striking Elbow

For close-in fighting, elbows can be used to both block or deflect a punching attack and for counterattacks: any block can double as a blow. Forcefully striking an attacking arm or leg with a block can send enough "referral shock" into the offending limb to paralyze muscles and break bones, in effect rendering the attacking arm or leg useless.

Knee and Leg Blocks

The rising knee and lower legs (shins) can be used for blocking, not only against kicks, but, depending on your flexibility, to block attacks to the abdomen. It is preferable to block an attacker's blade with a foot (kick) or with a deflecting knee since legs and feet are usually protected by (thick) pants and shoes. In addition, feet and legs themselves can generally take more punishment (stabs and cuts) than the arms (which will be needed for grappling should an attacker close in).

CHAPTER SEVEN

Assassin Blade Techniques and Strategy

We live in the age of the gun. But rather than making blades obsolete, the modern age's overdependence on firearms actually works to the blade wielder's advantage since an enemy may underestimate the lethal potential of the blade. For example, whereas most modern body armor designs will stop many handgun bullets, many won't stop a knife blade. This is because lead bullets expand on contact with body armor material, whereas knives (especially daggers and well-made combat knives) and other piercing instruments (high quality arrows, etc.) retain their shape and sharp edges. In the Middle Ages, Assassins studied how to circumvent crusader armor, learning that, whereas a long sword, spear, arrow, or other such weapon couldn't penetrate, a small dirk could.

Is there really that much difference between 14th century knight's armor and the Kevlar body armor of today? Not when it comes to quality edged weapons.

FIGHTERS VERSUS KILLERS

Medieval assassins were not trained to be knife fighters so much as simply to be killers. There is a big difference between having the mind-set of a knife *fighter* and having the mind-set of a knife *killer*. In prison, where homemade knives ("shanks") are the main weapon of necessity, convicts have a saying: "You never see the knife that kills you." According to prison logic, if one prisoner pulls a knife on a fellow prisoner and lets his intended victim see the knife, the first prisoner is just trying to scare the second prisoner. Conversely, a convict determined to kill another never lets the intended victim know he (the attacker) has a knife until the victim feels it enter his body. (Often a prisoner will feign friendship with the intended victim—an old assassin ploy—in order to get the victim to drop his guard.)

BLADE BASICS

Whereas some societies never developed the bow and arrow, all primitive societies developed knives, first as tools, then as weapons. Knives are the simplest of weapons to make. All you need is a sharp stick or a shard of obsidian. When man graduated from hunting animals to hunting his fellows, knives became more specialized, evolving into swords and other killing blades. From African fighting knives such as the Ethiopian *shotel* sword, the Dahomey *yekplenetoh* (straight razor), and the respected Zulu *assegai* (short spear) to the East Indian *katar* (punching dagger) and *bagh nakh* ("tiger claws"), Okinawan *sai* and *kama*, and the Japanese ninja's use of *shuriken* (throwing stars), societies and cultures developed specialized bladed weapons and often systemized styles of combat based on those weapons.

Ironically, while the world thinks of America as the land of the gun, American's first private martial arts school was founded in 1820s Louisiana, where there existed a studio where students learned knife-fighting techniques from Jim Bowie.

For the novice, the prospect of having to study the myriad of bladed weapons, not to mention the scores of knife-fighting styles and schools, is daunting. However, no matter what the particular type of knife, human anatomy limits the ways a knife can effectively be gripped and used. In other words, knifelike weapons must be held in one of two grips: the outside grip or the inside grip.

Outside Knife Grip

Using the outside grip (Illustration 8i), the knife is held with the blade extending out from the thumb side of the hand. An attacker stabs forward in a straight thrusting attack, targeting areas along the centerline if his opponent is facing him (Illustration 4) and into multiple targets along the spine and back when attacking

Illustration 8

from the rear (Illustration 5). The outside grip also allows for upward-rising stabs along the centerline, targeting the groin, solar plexus, or throat (Illustration 16), and slashing back and forth (inward toward his centerline and outward away from his centerline) along a horizontal plane, as well as up and down diagonally in an "X" pattern (Illustration 9).

Inside Knife Grip

When using the inside grip, the combatant holds the knife with the blade extending out from the bottom of the fist. This places the blade flush with the forearm, making it easier to conceal during pre-fight (Illustration 11). Attackers employing the inside grip tend to stab downward into the upper body of a victim, targeting the side of the neck and the subclavicle arteries. (This high-level, inside grip, downward slashing movement is the most common type of knife attack employed by the untrained.) The inside grip can also be used for back-and-forth slashing attacks along a horizontal plane (Illustration 14). Held flush along the forearm, a long-bladed knife or similarly elongated weapon can be used to reinforce a forearm block, such as when defending against an overhead bludgeon attack.

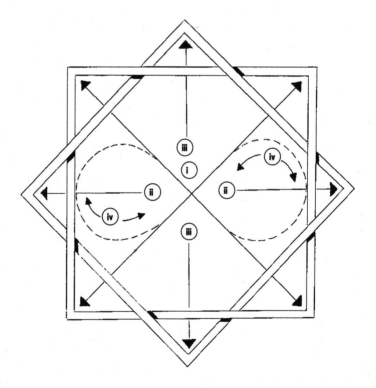

Illustration 9

• • • • •

Beginning students always ask how tightly they should grip their knife. The answer is traditional, yet still valid: hold your blade as if it were a little bird. Held too tightly, it will not be able to breathe; too loosely, and it will fly from your hand.

BASIC ATTACK PATTERNS

A knife fighter is restricted to a limited number of basic cuts or directions of attack, regardless of the grip he is using. These consist of straight-in stabs, inside-outside horizontal slashes, ascending-descending vertical slashes, and diagonal "X" slashes, also known as "figure 8s."

Untrained attackers often attempt straight-in stabs (Illustration 9i). On the other hand, experienced knife fighters often make thrusts toward a victim's face in order to elicit a flinch reaction.

Horizontal cuts (Illustration 9ii) slash back and forth along a horizontal line. (The untrained use such slashing at the level of their would-be victim's solar plexus, whereas skilled killers use horizontal cuts to attack a victim's throat from the front, pulling a victim off balance and cutting their throat before the victim even realizes a knife has been drawn.

Horizontal cuts can be made with the knife held in either the inside or outside grip. A double-edged knife can easily be drawn back and forth along this horizontal plane. A single-edged blade must be rotated by flipping the wrist each time it completes its inside or outside swing. Note: Care must be taken when using the horizontal cut to employ short slashes rather than overly wide swings that close off your centerline and leave you vulnerable to counterattack (Illustration 9iii.).

Vertical cuts rise up from the floor (using the outside grip) or slash down from overhead (using an inside grip). Note: Care must be taken when employing downward slashing strikes from the front, in order to avoid overextending the drawing back of your hand, thus opening yourself up to counter-jamming (Illustration 9iv).

Diagonal "X" cuts slash up and down in a crisscrossing motion. This type of cutting can be used with an up-and-back slashing action, or can be blended into a continuous figure-8 cutting pattern.

MOVEMENT RUSES, FEINTS, AND STRATAGEMS

Knowing *when* to use a weapon is just as important as knowing *how* to use that weapon. Say you have been cornered by an attacker in your own home. Behind your back you hold a ballpoint pen or a shard of broken glass (both viable knife substitutes) You know *how* to use your makeshift weapon—straight through the eye and into the brain—but unless you know *when* to strike, timing your single strike just right, your weapon will be useless.

Assassin recruits were taught to disguise both their intent to do bodily harm and the weapon with which they intended to do that bodily harm. Ideally, an assassin's victim never saw the assassin's weapon until he tasted blood.

The Veiled Hand

Professional knife fighters disguise the movement of their blades by keeping their free hand "dancing" in front of their blade hand. Intent on keeping track of the attacking blade each time the attacker's blade disappears and then reappears from behind the blocking hand, the defender's eyes and mind must readjust. The split second delay a defender's eyes and mind needs to readjust to the disappearance and reappearance of the threatening blade can be all the attacker needs to deliver the telling blow. Among assassins, this technique is known as the veiled hand.

Illustration 10i shows how the veiled hand allows the assassin to hide his blade's movement (up and down, side to side).

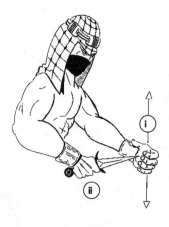

Illustration 10

94

Illustration 10ii shows how the veiled hand also permits the assassin to shift the knife unseen from an inside to an outside grip.

Concealing Your Weapons

Assassin sappers extrapolated the concept of the veiled hand to include larger weapons (swords, spears). Larger weapons could be hidden behind an assassin's body, even when the assassin was not wearing a voluminous robe or cloak. Carrying weapons flush with or behind his body also helped distort his silhouette at night.

Modern-day assassins and street thugs know the advantange of

Illustration 11

Illustration 12

concealing weapons in order to get close to an intended victim without alerting that victim to danger. For example, that harmless looking drunk staggering toward you appears to be carrying a bottle in a paper bag. But, even if the paper bag is in the shape of a bottle, how can you be *certain* there is a bottle in it?

Carefully concealed weapons are often missed during a curso-

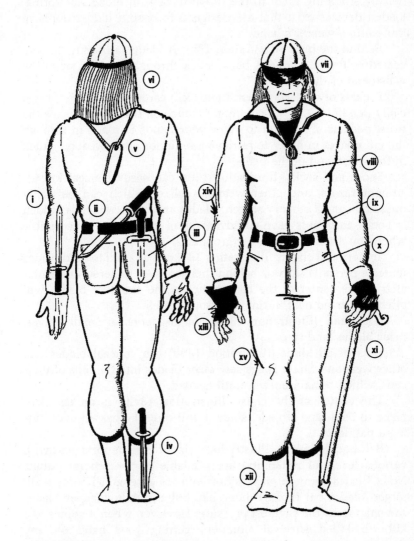

Illustration 13

ry search. As a result, street punks and other killers have mastered the art of concealing deadly blades.

Up-the-sleeve (Illustration 13i): A variety of knives can be hidden by strapping them to the forearm. Several models of spring-loaded devices exist that are designed to drop a hidden forearm knife into a wearer's hand.

Behind-the-back (Illustration 13ii): A blade can easily be concealed behind a wielder's back, stuck through the belt, or in the waistband of the pants.

Pockets of all sorts (Illustration 13iii) can conceal blades, especially pen knives. It is a common practice on the street to slice the waist pockets of a jacket to allow your hands to reach in through the cut pocket in order to retrieve a knife (or other weapon) stuck in the waistband of the pants.

Shoes and socks (Illustration 13iv) can easily conceal knives, straight razors, and other weapons, all of which can be easily missed during a cursory search. Blades and other weapons hidden in socks and boots have an advantage of being readily accessible when you are knocked to the ground.

Tethers and chains (Illustration 13v) can be used to hold blades under a person's shirt or behind their back. A tethered knife situated in the center of the back between the shoulder blades will often be passed over during a cursory search.

Long hair (Illustration 13vi) can also conceal small knives, razor blades, and so on.

Hats of all kinds (Illustration 13vii) can conceal blades and other weapons. Street gangs sew razor blades into the bills of their caps, which remain unseen until needed.

The center of the chest (Illustration 13viii) is an excellent place to duct-tape a blade, since it will often be passed over during a pat-down.

Belt-buckle knives (Illustration 13ix) of various sorts (and with various levels of reliability) are available to the general public. Note: Blades come in an array of tempers (strengths). Some well-forged blades cut through bone like butter, while cheaper blades can snap from the slightest pressure. However, when it comes to a kill-or-be-killed survival situation, getting your hand on any weapon—a cheap blade or otherwise—is better than being unarmed. Snowball better than no ball!

The groin area (Illustration 13x) is an excellent place to hide a blade, since most security personnel will pass over the groin rather than grope it during a pat-down search. (Note: This does not apply to security personnel in San Francisco.)

Canes and umbrellas (Illustration 13xi) can make excellent spearing weapons. Sword canes of assorted types (and levels of reliability) are also available. Street gangs often augment canes and umbrellas by sharpening the points.

Boots (Illustration 13xii) worn by gang members are often augmented with protruding spikes. Legal-to-wear cleats (further sharpened by street thugs) are a definite asset in any kill-or-be-killed situation, whether or not the wearer is an accomplished kicker.

Gloves (Illustration 13xiii) can be affixed with protruding spikes to augment punching. Sharpened, such spikes can cause major damage or death from blood loss. Street gangs sew razor blades onto the fingers and seams of gloves between the thumb and index finger. This arrangement allows an attacker to cut a victim's throat simply by seizing their throat.

Elbows (Illustration 13iv) can be augmented with spikes attached to elbow pads on the jacket. These spikes supplement elbow blows and, if of sufficient length, can kill.

Knees are likewise augmented with spike-impregnated knee pads (Illustration 13xv) worn under the pants. These spikes can cause severe damage when directed against a victim's groin, causing bleeding, trauma, and shock. They can also be used against a victim's head (pressed downward by your hands) to stun, causing unconsciousness or death.

CHAPTER EIGHT

Movement Patterns

It is instinctual for humans to move back and away from danger. While this reflex gets us out of trouble most of the time, today's experienced attackers familiar with these instinctual reactions use them against their victims, just as medieval Assassins once used such instincts against their targets. Janna combat training taught Assassin trainees to step toward and into an opponent, since it is unnatural to step toward danger and is the last thing an opponent—especially an armed attacker—expects.

UP AND DOWN

It is instinctual to duck when a threat is aimed at your head. Unfortunately, just ducking seldom gets us out of danger (Illustration 14i).

When used for self-defense, ducking must be a purposeful action designed to get us out of danger or to help us overcome an attacker. Any ducking action must be followed up with a counteraction, either fleeing or counterattacking.

Likewise, when something threatens our lower body, we jump up. For most people, jumping up (to avoid a leg sweep, etc.) is not instinctual and must be trained, like jumping rope. An attacking assassin comes in low under an opponent's guard or attacking hand to strike or counterstrike into an opponent's body.

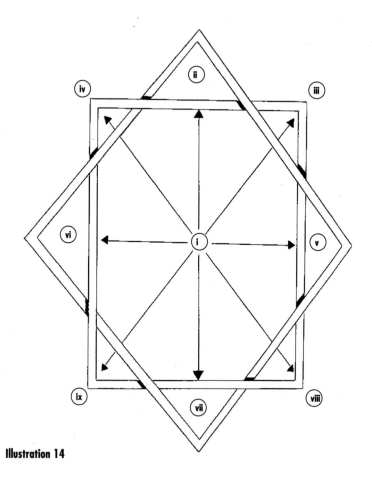

Illustration 14

BACK-STEP STRAIGHT

It is also instinctive to backpedal when faced with an attacker. Unfortunately, merely backpedaling to the rear still permits an attacker to continue his straight-line attack. For the purpose of offensive action, it is important to learn to step backwards (Illustration 14ii) without losing your balance in order to draw a grappling opponent off balance (in preparation for a throwing technique or for impaling him on a blade).

BACK-STEP DIAGONAL LEFT

When stepping back (Illustration 14iii), it is preferable to step back diagonally. Stepping back diagonally places you at an oblique angle to your opponent and puts you in position for a throwing technique or for a counterattack. Against a straight forward advancing opponent, stepping diagonally throws off his advance, causing momentary hesitation as he must adjust to your new position.

BACK-STEP DIAGONAL RIGHT

This works the same as backpedaling left (Illustration 14iv). The choice of direction is made to place yourself in the most advantageous position for throwing and counterstriking.

SIDE-SHIFT LEFT

This allows you to move to the outside of an attacker's thrusting hand or foot (Illustration 14v), placing you in a better position for counterattacking with a hand blow (targeting the attacker's centerline) or with a foot strike (a side kick or a sweeping-in kick). This shift also places you in a better position for slicing across your opponent's body using a horizontal blade stroke (see Illustration Nine).

SIDE-SHIFT RIGHT

Whether to shift right or left depends on your attacker's thrust, since you want to move to the outside of his power (Illustration 14vi).

FORWARD-STEP STRAIGHT

Meeting an attacker head-on is seldom a good idea, since his strategy for attacking you straight-on depends on your remaining in the path of his punches, kicks, or weapon thrusts (Illustration 14vii).

Stepping straight forward is effective for jamming an attacker's punches and kicks before he can effectively execute them. The surprise of stepping forward to meet an attacker must be weighed against the danger of meeting an attack head-on.

FORWARD-STEP DIAGONAL LEFT

Ideally, when countering a straight forward attack, you should move forward diagonally (Illustration 14viii), shifting forward either to the right or left. This shifting forward places you in the ideal position for counterattacking (see Illustration 15).

FORWARD-STEP DIAGONAL RIGHT

The same advice applies as for a side shift (Illustration 14ix).

COUNTERATTACKING

When faced with a kill-or-be-killed situation, any movement on your part must be intended to first, take you out of the "line of fire" and second, place you in the best position to counterattack.

Faced with an attacker, the defender blocks the attacking hand (or foot) in toward the attacker's centerline (Illustration 15i), while simultaneously stepping diagonally forward (Illustration 15ii), which takes the defender out of the line of fire and forces the attacker to hesitate in order to redirect his attack. Any hesitation on the attacker's part, allows the defender time (if only a second) to counterattack or flee past the attacker. The defender counterattacks with blows directed into the attacker's side or centerline (Illustration 15iii), or uses a sweeping hand movement to unbalance the attacker.

Note: A defender's counterattack is aided by seizing and retaining control of the attacker's thrusting hand or foot.

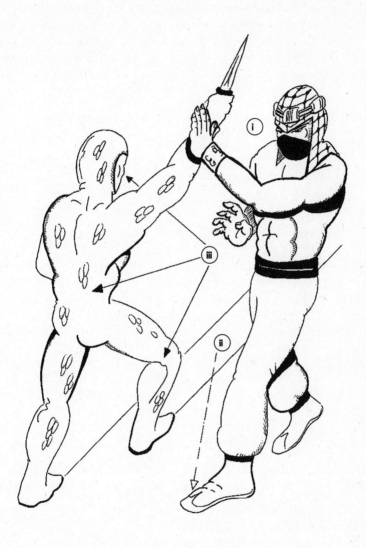

Illustration 15

CHAPTER NINE

Targeting and Anatomy

"The more you know about how the human body is put together, the easier it is to take it apart."

—Dirk Skinner,
*Street Ninja: Ancient Secrets
for Today's Mean Streets*

BLADE LENGTHS AND STRENGTHS

Even a small knife can kill. A razor blade is barely an inch long, yet think of the damage a simple double-edged razor blade can do to the human body. A three-inch long blade (legal in most places) is more than sufficient to kill a human being. Longer blades, on the other hand, have the advantage of doing more damage to underlying organs (organs behind the actual organ you are targeting).

Many blade schools train students to twist their blades after stabbing into a victim in order to do maximum damage. However, twisting a knife in a wound should only be done when you are assured of the quality of your knife. A well-tempered blade will stand up to such twisting, while a cheap blade will snap in two in the wound.

Snapping a blade off in a victim's wound is counterproductive, since it helps prevent blood loss by blocking the wound. If you hit what your aiming at in the first place, there is no need to twist your blade.

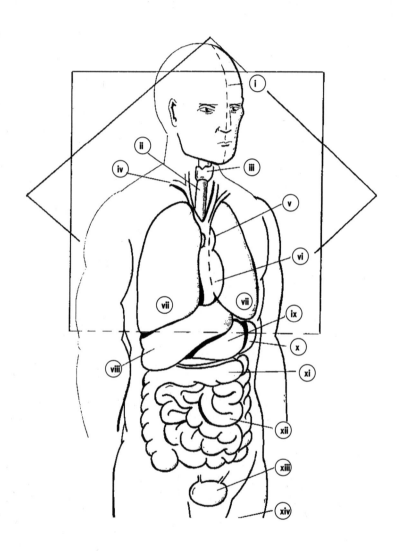

Illustration 16

FRONTAL TARGETS

The front of the body offers many viable and effective targets.

Centerline
Martial artists envision an imaginary line running down the center of their bodies (Illustration 16i), running between the eyes, down the front of the torso to the testicles (balanced on both sides). Martial arts students are taught to guard their own centerline while attacking their opponent's.

Throat and Neck
Attack the throat and neck area (Illustration 16ii) from the front using stabbing thrusts and horizontal slashes. (Refer to Illustration 17 for a more detailed discussion of the inner organs of the throat and neck.)

Larynx
(See Illustrations 16iii and 17vi.)

Aorta
The aorta (Illustration 16v) and the arteries branching off from it carry blood away from the heart to the brain and extremities. The ascending aorta, situated at the top of the heart, is attacked using a rising vertical stroke stabbing in and up at the solar plexus. This target can also be attacked by striking down into the hollow of the neck between the clavicles. Severing it causes unconsciousness in 30 seconds and death within three minutes due to the interruption of blood flow to the brain.

Heart
Any major trauma to the heart (sudden penetration, forceful blow) can stop it from beating. When the heart (Illustration 16vi) stops beating, blood ceases to flow to the extremities (such as the brain), which cease to function. Surprise! You're dead.

The heart is well protected by the rib cage and the sternum and is further insulated by the lungs. It is best attacked by striking (hand blow or knife) up and into the solar plexus.

Lungs

While not immediately fatal, a preliminary knife strike to either lung (Illustration 16vii), coming up and under the solar plexus, makes it difficult for a victim to breathe and can cause unconsciousness (due to trauma). Lung strikes are used as softening-up blows designed to make the victim susceptible to the coup de grace.

Liver

A forceful hand blow to the liver (Illustration 16viii) area can cause pain, internal bleeding and unconsciousness (due to trauma). A knife strike to the liver can cause unconsciousness and death.

Stomach

Stomach wounds (Illustration 19ix) are painful, but not immediately fatal (though victims have died from trauma and shock). For Assassins, the stomach is more of a softening-up strike. The stomach is attacked using straight-in stabs with rising vertical slashes and horizontal cuts (see Illustration nine).

Spleen

Trauma (blows, stabs, and cuts) to the spleen (Illustration 19x) causes pain, unconsciousness, and even death. Attack the spleen with forceful hand blows and with straight-in jabs. Horizontal cuts can be employed after shifting to the victim's left side (see Illustrations 14 and 15).

Large Intestine

While not immediately fatal, stabs and cuts to the large intestine (Illustration 16xi) cause pain, unconscious, and sometimes death (due to blood loss and trauma). If unarmed, use forceful hand and foot blows. Armed with a knife, target this organ with straight-in stabs, rising vertical slashes, horizontal cuts, and low-level diagonal cuts.

Small Intestine

Long blades can stab into and through the small intestine (Illustration 16xii) if the stab is deep enough and reaches into the arteries and veins supplying blood to kidneys (see IIllustration 19).

Bladder

Hand, foot, and knife strikes to the bladder (Illustration 16xiii) are painful, but not immediately fatal. Still, blows to the bladder can cause pain and unconsciousness (due to trauma). If you are unarmed, attack the bladder with low-level rising kicks and stomps. With a blade, employ rising vertical stabs.

Groin

Hand and foot strikes to the groin can cause distraction, pain, and unconsciousness. While not immediately fatal, knife strikes to the groin area cause pain, bleeding, and unconsciousness (due to fear and trauma). Blade attacks to the groin use rising vertical stabs.

Major (femoral) arteries run up both the inner thighs. Severing one of these arteries causes major blood loss that can result in unconsciousness and, if left untreated, death due to blood loss.

TARGETING THE MAJOR VESSELS

It has been said that an adventure is a result of incompetence. This holds true for assassins. If an assassin has to struggle with an opponent, something has gone wrong. Let's examine how this applies to knife fighting.

A knife fighter can afford to wear an opponent down by fencing with him until the opponent drops from a loss of blood or until authorities arrive to break up the fight.

With few exceptions, even striking into a major artery will not instantly kill an opponent. Though you succeed in severing a major artery, an opponent may still be able to kill you before he bleeds to death. More often than not, in the heat of battle, a knife fighter will not even realize he has been seriously cut until after the excitement of the fight wanes. All too often, in a protracted knife fight, it's the man who bleeds slowest who wins!

An assassin is not a fighter. Implicit in the nature of an assassin's business was the necessity of getting in and out as quickly as possible. The longer the assassin had to spend on enemy ground, the higher the likelihood of his mission being compromised. In other words, assassins didn't have time to waste in fencing with a sentry. Nonetheless, assassins had to be prepared for any contingency. If a single, telling cut could not be delivered, the assassin might have to settle for inflicting a fatal wound on his target, severing a major artery so the victim would bleed to death, or allowing the poison on the assassin's blade to do its job.

Arteries carry blood away from the heart out to vital organs and extremities. Veins carry blood back to the heart to pick up needed oxygen. Severing one of these arteries or veins can be compared to cutting the supply lines to an army in the field: without needed ammunition and supplies (arterial blood) being ferried out to them, an army in the field grinds to a halt. Likewise, without intelligence (veinous blood) coming in on a regular basis, the commander (heart) has no idea what is needed out in the field.

By the way, dull knife blades collapse arteries, helping staunch blood loss. Conversely, a sharp knife cleanly severs arteries and veins, allowing blood to flow freely.

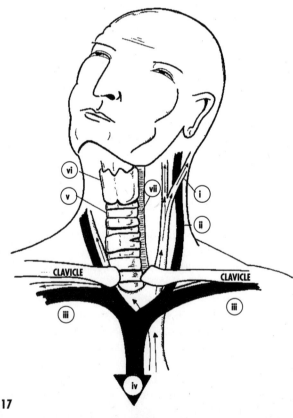

Illustration 17

Neck Arteries

Since neck arteries (Illustration 17i) carry blood to the brain, severing one (such as the carotid artery, situated on both sides of the neck under the ear) causes unconsciousness and death within seconds. In lieu of a blade, a forceful open-hand blow to the side of the neck forces blood out of the neck arteries, producing a "blood-spurt" into an opponent's brain that causes temporary disorientation or unconsciousness.

Neck Veins

We know that veins carry blood back to the heart. Severing a major vein (such as the jugular, running roughly parallel to the carotid artery) causes unconsciousness and death (due to blood loss, trauma, and heart arrest).

Subclavian arteries (Illustration 17iii) carry blood to the arms. Severing one of these arteries diverts blood from the brain, causing unconsciousness in seconds and death within three minutes. Subclavian arteries can also be severed by a forceful blow (hand or bludgeon) that breaks the clavicle bone and forces the splintered bone down to perforate the sub-clavicle artery. Heavy bludgeon blows can also be used for this purpose.

TARGETING THE THROAT

Trachea

The trachea (aka the windpipe) connects the mouth and nose with the lungs (Illustration 17v) and is vital for breathing. Severing the trachea, while not immediately fatal, will severely interfere with a victim's breathing.

Larynx

Attack the larynx (aka voice box and Adam's apple; Illustration 17vi) with forceful hand or bludgeon blows (designed to crush the larynx) and with slashing knife strokes (designed to sever the larynx). A crushed larynx blocks the trachea, preventing the victim from breathing. Unconsciousness and death from asphyxia occurs within minutes unless an emergency tracheotomy is performed to open the trachea below the blockage.

Note: Crushing the larynx is one of the most effective ways of strangling a victim.

Esophagus

Slashing deeply into the throat can sever both the trachea (windpipe) and the esophagus (food tube to the stomach; Illustration 17vii). Severing the esophagus, while not in and of itself fatal, causes trauma and blood loss sufficient to produce pain, unconsciousness (due to trauma and shock), and death (due to blood loss).

TARGETING THE HEAD

Though protected by the helmet of the skull, the brain can be attacked through several openings ("gates"). Assassin recruits were taught that the proper way of striking a victim was to visualize a target behind the actual target. For example, if your intent is to stab into the intestine, visualize your blade coming out the victim's back. Likewise, when punching into an opponent's face, visualize your fist driving through the victim's head and coming out the back of his skull.

Eyes

Any rigid object (a conventional knife, blunt stick, rigid fingers) can be shoved through the eye (Illustration 18i) and into the brain to kill a victim. Even a half-hearted strike to the eyes can elicit a flinch reaction, pain, and temporary blindness.

Target the eye socket with straight-in knife jabs, downward vertical stabs (when a victim's head has been pulled back), and rising stabs (when a victim's head has been pressed down).

Nose

During close-in grappling, target the nasal socket (Illustration 18ii) with stiff fingers (causing pain, tearing of the eyes, and choking due to bleeding). Target up through the nasal opening with rising vertical knife stabs or with straight-in stabs when the head has been pulled back.

Mouth

Target the mouth (Illustration 18iii) with forceful unarmed and bludgeon blows designed to break teeth, causing pain, bleeding, and possible choking from broken teeth lodging in the throat. Stab through the mouth opening, up into the brain. Note: Any stab into the open mouth can cause severe damage to the tissue of the palate

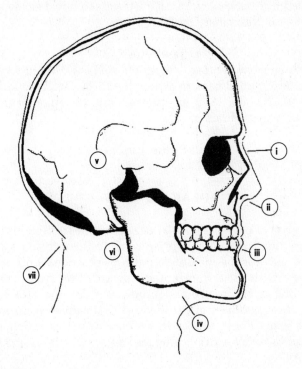

Illustration 18

and the pharynx (back of the throat), resulting in trauma and shock, bleeding, and choking (asphyxiation).

Chin

Target up under the chin (into the upper throat; Illustration 18iv) with rising vertical stabs and with straight-in stabs when the head has been pulled back to expose the neck.

Ears

Target the brain by stabbing in through the ears with a thin stabbing weapon (ice pick, ballpoint pen, etc.). Even if the weapon isn't of sufficient length to penetrate the brain, stabbing into the delicate muscles of the inner ear causes great pain, disorientation, and unconsciousness. Note: The center of balance in the human body is in the ears. A forceful open-hand slap to the ears can unbalance a victim. Attackers often use just such an unbalancing slap as a softening-up preliminary strike.

Jawbone

Attacking from the rear or from the side angle when a victim's head has been pulled back to expose the throat, stab up under the jawbone (Illustration 18vi) to penetrate into the spine or into the medulla oblongata (brain stem).

Skull-Spine Juncture

See Illustration 19.

REAR TARGETS

It is always preferable to attack a victim from behind. Not only does the element of surprise work to the attacker's advantage, but most of a person's natural weapons and natural defensive motions are oriented toward the front, making approaching a victim from behind safer for the attacker. In addition, few people train to defend themselves from attacks from the rear. These lapses in defense work as much to the advantage of today's street mugger as they did assassins in the Middle Ages.

The Base of the Skull

This is an excellent target for hand blows and weapon strikes. Any forceful hand blow (hammer blow, palm blow) or heavy bludgeon strike to this area (Illustration 19i) will result in pain, unconsciousness, and possible death from blunt trauma or a broken neck. Thrust through this gate with a blade to sever the spinal cord (where it meets the brain stem) or pierce the brain itself. This is a much prized target when removing a sentry.

The Seventh Vertebra

(See Illustrations 19ii and 20ii.)

The Kidneys

A forceful unarmed blow or bludgeon strike to the kidneys (Illustration 19iii) produces pain, unconsciousness, internal bleeding, and sometimes death. With a blade, strike up into

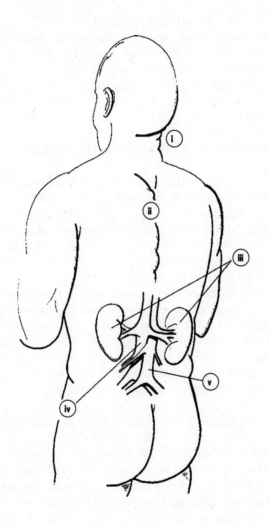

Illustration 19

117

the kidneys with a rising vertical strike/outside grip to cause instant unconsciousness and death.

Renal Artery and Vein

Target the major renal artery (Illustration 19iv) and major renal vein (Illustration 19v)—situated between the two kidneys, under the spine—by cutting through the spine (damaging the spine in the process) or at an oblique angle, avoiding the bone of the spine. Severing either of these blood pathways results in the death of the victim.

ADDITIONAL SPINAL CORD TARGETS

The brain sends marching orders to the rest of the body via the spinal cord. Attacking the spinal cord nerves is analogous to guerrillas cutting telephone lines in preparation for attacking a garrison; without the ability to call for reinforcements and with no way to receive orders, the garrison is lost. In the same way, any damage to the vital spinal cord destroys the brain's line of communication to the rest of the body.

Any forceful intrusion into a spinal area destroys the functioning of the areas (muscles, organs, etc.) controlled by those particular spinal nerves. In other words, damage to the spinal cord causes loss of body function below the injury level. For example, a man fracturing his fifth cervical vertebra might lose the use of his triceps, hands, chest, leg, and lower body muscles. Damage to the fourth cervical vertebra can paralyze respiration: can't breathe, can't fight.

Victims of spinal trauma become subject to secondary systems shut-down (such as kidney failure) once the communications lines from the brain that kept them functioning are severed.

The spinal cord's nerves are divided into four areas. In descending order they are: cervical nerves (eight), thoracic nerves (12), lumbar nerves (five), and sacral nerves (five).

Skull

The brain and spinal column connect at the base of the skull (Illustration 20i) and can be attacked with forceful hand blows and with heavy bludgeon blows to produce unconsciousness and death. Heavy blows to this area can break the neck of a victim,

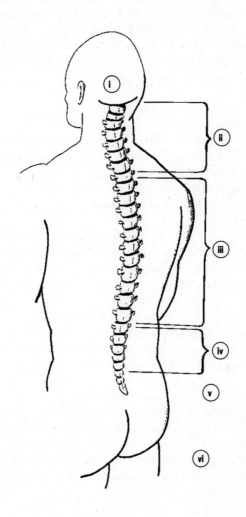

Illustration 20

119

paralyzing or killing him. Spinal trauma to this area is especially telling, since it can paralyze everything below the point of injury. Violent wrenching of the neck can also result in pain, unconsciousness, and death due to referral shock to the spinal column. Blade strikes up into the base of the skull cause paralysis due to spinal nerve damage and death (by penetrating into the brain or paralyzing heart and lung function).

Cervical Nerves

These nerves (Illustration 20ii) control the head and neck, arm and hand muscles, and the diaphragm, which is necessary for breathing. The seventh vertebra (between the shoulder blades) is a common target for descending vertical knife strikes with an outside grip. Successful penetration of the seventh vertebra causes paralysis, unconsciousness, and death.

Thoracic Nerves

The thoracic nerves (Illustration 20iii) control the chest and abdominal muscles. Strikes to this portion of the spinal column produce pain and interfere with upper body motor function.

Lumbar Nerves

These nerves (Illustration 20iv) control the use of the legs. A forceful attack into the spine at this area can paralyze a victim's legs and lower body.

Sacral Nerves

These control the bowels, bladder, sexual function, and the feet. While not a prime blade target, striking up into the sacral area (Illustration 20v) with a forceful kick from behind can be an excellent softening-up and unbalancing strike. A forceful strike to the tailbone (coccyx) area causes extreme pain and interferes with the opponent's mobility.

Rectum and Groin

While not an immediately fatal target, stabbing up into a victim's rectum or groin (Illustration 20vi) from behind (a rising vertical cut with an outside grip) elicits pain, bleeding, or unconsciousness (due to fear and trauma).

Note: Burying a blade (no matter how small) in an attacker's groin and leaving it there destroys an opponent's mobility, allowing you time to flee or to deliver the finishing blow.

CHAPTER TEN

Knife Attack Techniques

The perfect knife victim stands completely still, arms spread wide, allowing you to bury your blade up through the his solar plexus to his heart, killing him instantly. Unfortunately, from the Assassin's point of view at least, the perfect victim seldom presents himself.

Human beings instinctively protect themselves by backpedaling, thrashing their arms about, or running like hell so that only rear targets present themselves to your blade. Infused with a rush of adrenaline, fighting for survival, the body of even an untrained human being is capable of putting up formidable resistance even when the mind of that human being is drowning in panic. How much more so the body of a *trained* fighter?

FRONTAL ATTACKS

It is always preferable to approach a victim from the rear. However, there are times when targeted individuals must be attacked from the front. No matter how undesirable, a trained Assassin must study for any and all eventualities.

Approaching a victim from the front, the victim will not know the Assassin intends him harm until the Assassin's blade has tasted his blood.

When attacking into an opponent's front, use softening-up techniques (Illustration 21i) to distract and unbalance your victim, setting him up for the final blow. Softening-up techniques include

Illustration 21

feinting high while striking low, throwing something into the victim's eyes (eliciting a flinch reaction or blinding him), attacking him with stomps and sweeps to the legs, and with the old tried-and-true knee to the groin.

The ideal front knife strike (rising vertical with an outside grip) targets up through the solar plexus straight into the heart (Illustrations 16vi and 21ii).

Stabbing into the intestines (Illustrations 21iii) with an outside grip, draw the knife upward, in effect bisecting the victim's abdomen.

It is often necessary to seize a hold on the victim's clothing or body (hair, head, arm; Illsutration 21iv) in order to prevent their backpedaling or to draw them forward onto your blade. Seizing the victim's head allows you to pull his head down into striking range, facilitating your to attack through one of the openings in the head.

Illustration 22

A solid palm blow under an opponent's chin (Illustration 22v) forces his head back, exposing the vulnerable throat and under-chin area to attack.

REAR ATTACKS

The rear approach increases the likelihood of surprise and shock to the target, while decreasing danger to the attacker.

Illustration 23

The respected technique for approaching a target, such as a sentry, is to approach to within three to five feet of the victim by employing a zigzag pattern (Illustration 23i). Trainees are warned not to look directly at an enemy sentry as they creep close to him since many believe that humans have a sixth sense about being watched. While this extrasensory ability to sense danger is still debated, it is always better to watch the sentry out of the corner of your eye and concentrate on where you are stepping so as not to give yourself away by stepping on a dry stick or loose gravel.

Having approached to within three to five feet of the target, the Assassin rushes across the remaining distance to attack the sentry. Reportedly British commandos were taught this technique by captured Thuggee who, in turn, derived their attack technique from observing Bengal tigers stalking prey.

Coming up behind the victim (Illustration 23ii), the Assassin stuns and silences the victim by slapping a hand over his mouth or by striking into the victim's exposed throat. Slapping your hand across the victim's mouth also allows you to pull the victim backward and off balance.

Note: Clasping your hand over the victim's mouth and nose causes him to instinctively raise his hands towards his face, which in turn opens his abdomen, sides, ribs, and armpits to attack.

Having secured a hold on the victim (Illustration 23iii), draw him back off balance and at the same time drive your blade into a primary rear target.

Note: In lieu of a bladed weapon, unarmed blows (fists, palm blows, elbows) can be used to target the kidneys, spine, and other targets along the back.

Having secured a hold on the victim (Illustration 23iv), draw him off balance by moving slightly back and dropping your weight while simultaneously pulling him with your other hand (the one covering his mouth or gripping his throat). For recalcitrant victims, stomp into the back of the knee.

Over-The-Shoulder Rear Attack

Approaching the victim from behind (Illustration 24i), slap your hand around the target's mouth and nose, and then violently jerk his head back and to the side.

Note: Jerking the head in this manner can wrench the

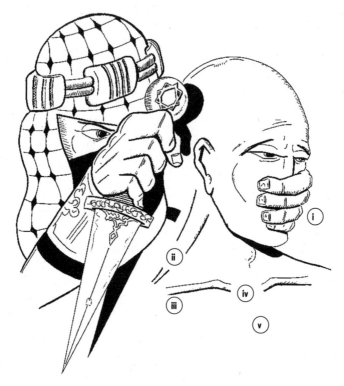

Illustration 24

neck, resulting in unconsciousness (from trauma) and death (from spinal separation).

Jerking the head to the side (Illustration 24ii) exposes the neck and throat to descending vertical stabs targeting the veins and arteries of the neck and the inner organs of the throat.

Stab down in front of and behind the clavicles (Illustration 24iii) to severe the subclavian arteries and veins.

Target the aorta and heart veins by attacking down into the exposed hollow of the throat (Illustration 24iv; between the clavicles).

After pulling the victim back (Illustration 24v), the heart can be attacked directly by thrusting down through the hollow of the throat or by thrusting upwards from under the solar plexus.

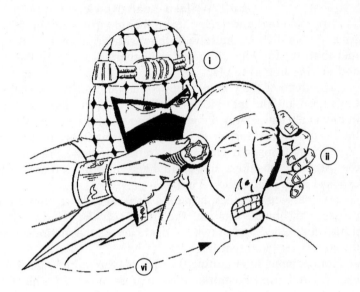

Illustration 25

Illustration 26

Butt 'n Slash Rear Attack

Approaching undetected from behind (Illustration 25i), the Assassin (holding his knife with the inside grip) smashes the pommel (butt) of his knife into the right temple, stunning the victim and driving him to the left.

The force of the pommel blow (Illustration 25ii) drives the victim's head left and into the grasp of the Assassin's left hand, which immediately clasps over the victim's mouth and nose and wrenches the head back and farther to the left, exposing the victim's throat.

Simultaneous to his left hand wrenching the victim's head left, the Assassin positions his knife hand in front of the victim's exposed neck (Illustration 25iii).

As the victim's neck is pulled back and down, the Assassin presses his blade against the front of the victim's throat (Illustration 25iv) and draws his blade across the victim's exposed throat, slicing his throat from left to right.

Immediately after cutting the victim's throat, the Assassin uses his left hand grip (Illustration 25v) to press the victim's head down onto the victim's chest to prevent noise (gurgling) from escaping from the severed windpipe.

Illustration 27

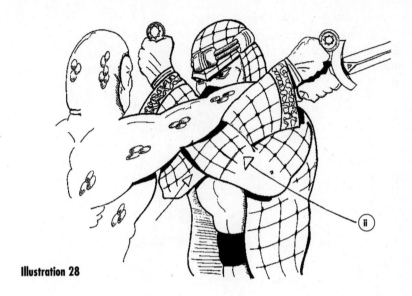

Illustration 28

ADDITIONAL ASSASSIN ATTACK TECHNIQUES

Even when attacking from the front, it is preferable to conceal your weapon from the intended target until the moment comes to strike. When the targeted enemy knows that the Assassin has a weapon, the fact that the enemy cannot see that weapon and keep track of it helps unnerve him.

While the enemy is trying to find the Assassin's hidden weapon, the victim is less likely to notice a subtle shifting of the feet.

The "Snake" Technique

Modern undercover agents all know the importance of carrying a back-up weapon and Assassins knew the value of this precaution back in the Middle Ages. In addition, Assassins developed techniques employing the use of two knives. These techniques were collectively known as "snake" techniques since the use of two knives brought to mind the fangs of a venomous serpent.

One advantage of filling each hand with a weapon is that the enemy doesn't know whether the attack will come from the left hand, the right hand, or both.

131

Illustration 29

Illustration 30   132

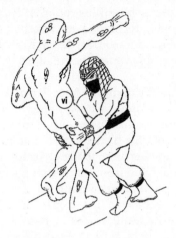

Illustration 31

When either approaching a targeted enemy or facing off against an attacker, the assassin operative employs a deceptive stance (Illustration 27i) that permits him to conceal his two blades (or substitute weapons) behind his back (up his sleeves, etc.).

Responding to an enemy's thrusting attack, the Assassin brings his hands forward and up to form a crossed-at-the-forearms X-block (Illustration 28ii) that deflects the enemy's thrusting attack and forces the enemy's arm higher, exposing his trunk to attack.

Note: In the event the Assassin is the aggressor, the overt act of flashing the blades upward will cause the enemy to raise his arms in a reflexive defensive move. This achieves the same desired effect—causing the enemy to expose his mid-body to attack. This X-block can also be employed sans weapons to block and trap unarmed punching attacks and to block weapons attacks.

Having succeeded in deflecting the enemy's attacking arm upward, the Assassin strikes into the enemy's exposed mid-body (Illustration 29iii) from one or both sides.

Should the enemy succeed in countering one of the Assassin's thrusts, the second still finds it's mark (Illustration 29iv).

This two-handed snake technique can also be used as an unarmed attack to counterstrike into an attacker's exposed sides (Illustration 30v) with bludgeon fists or elbow blows.

Having countered into the attacker's mid-body with elbow and hammer fist blows, drop your striking hands to sweep the attacker's legs out from under him (Illustration 31vi).

Note: this sweeping technique can also be employed by substituting a knife blade for the scooping hand. Knife-blade sweeps have the added advantage of severing the tendons behind the knee.

The Janna "Scorpion" Arm-Trap Technique

When closing to grapple with an enemy, an Assassin fighter used powerful grips on his opponent in order to unbalance or impale the enemy onto his blade. Assassin janna combat classified these grappling (trapping and locking) techniques as "scorpion" techniques, a term derived from the scorpion's use of claws to hold prey while striking with its venomous tail stinger.

This scorpion technique has a parallel in overall assassin strategy where the Assassin works in two-man teams, with one Assassin acting as the claws of the scorpion (seizing the victim) while the second Assassin (the venomous tail) delivers the coup de grace.

The attacking or defending assassin adopts a deceptive (behind the back) outside knife grip (Illustration 32i).

Once the attacking or defending enemy commits himself to a thrusting attack, the Assassin counters by turning into the attacking arm (Illustration 32ii) with a blocking/striking forearm blow.

Simultaneous to the blocking forearm blow, the Assassin seizes a grip on the enemy's thrusting forearm (Illustration 32iii).

When defending against a leading hand or leading foot attack, the Assassin must always beware of an enemy's rear follow-up hand (Illustration 32iv) or foot, since his leading hand attack might be a feint for his true rear hand attack.

Using the momentum of his turning inward for the forearm block, the assassin pivots on his lead foot (Illustration 32v), bringing his trailing foot around on the outside of his leading foot.

If necessary, the Assassin uses his leading foot (Illustration 32vi) to upset the balance of an attacker by employing an inward sweeping kick, targeting the enemy's leading leg.

Having blocked an enemy's thrusting hand, the Assassin slides his hand down to the enemy's forearm (Illustration 33vii) to seize the enemy's wrist and hand.

Firmly digging his thumb into the back of the attacker's hand (Illustration 33viii) while digging his fingers into the base of the

Illustration 32

thumb (palm), the Assassin wrenches the enemy's hand in a counterclockwise direction, causing the enemy to drop his weapon or breaking the enemy's wrist, retaining his grip on the enemy's wrist (Illustration 34ix).

The assassin drapes his elbow over the enemy's extended arm (Illustration 34x), trapping the attacking arm by locking out the elbow in the armpit.

Retaining his dual grip at the wrist and elbow, the Assassin continues his pivot inward (Illustration 34xi) and attacks into the enemy's exposed side (Illustration 34xii) as the enemy is drawn forward and thrown off balance by the assassin's double lock at his wrist and elbow.

Note: This technique can also be employed as an effective unarmed combat technique by substituting pivoting-in elbow srikes to the side (ribs) and the side of the head (targeting the temple) of a trapped enemy.

Second note: Once the wrist-elbow double lock has been established, merely falling on the victim's arm will drive him to the ground or break his elbow. Extend your leg as you pull your opponent around and down by applying the arm pressure. This will cause him to trip over your extended leg.

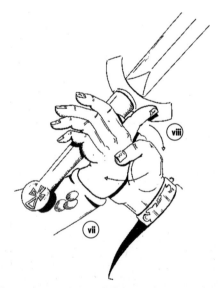

Illustration 33

Illustration 34

CHAPTER ELEVEN

Janna Self-Defense Awareness

Vigilance is always your first and last line of defense. Being aware of yourself and your surroundings is the key to survival in any time and clime.

The number one thing all human predators look for in potential victims is a lapse in awareness. Where street predators do not spot natural distraction in their targeted victims, they create distractions by asking their victims for the time or asking for directions and then sucker-punch the victim when the victim glances away.

There are three aspects to awareness: awareness of self, awareness of your surroundings, and awareness of your enemy.

AWARENESS OF SELF

This entails a realistic assessment of your mental and physical abilities. Do you have the physical skills and cunning to defeat an attacker? If you can not fight him off, can you scare him off? What is his motivation? Is he after money or is he after *you*?

Overestimating yourself can be just as lethal as underestimating an attacker. Get to know yourself, your strengths, weaknesses, and fears. Become friends with your body and discipline your mind, and they will work together to safely see you through any danger.

AWARENESS OF SURROUNDINGS

Awareness also requires realistically assessing a situation. In some street confrontations, it is to your advantage to delay an attacker until help arrives. At other times, delay works to your attacker's benefit. The assessment of a situation includes limiting the time you spend in under-lighted, economically depressed areas of the city.

Make yourself aware of the potential environmental weapons and defensive obstacles your surroundings offer you.

AWARENESS OF YOUR ENEMY

Finally, being aware means always remembering that, despite all your plans and martial arts training—after all your praying to Jesus (or Allah, as the case may be)—shit happens! Train to improvise. Survival of the fittest dictates that those best able to realistically assess changing conditions and then adjust are the fittest and therefore the most apt to survive. Simple, no?

BLOCKERS, OBSTACLES,
AND KNIFE SUBSTITUTES

There is an oft repeated saying, "Keep your friends close and your enemies closer!" Strategy-wise, this is good advice. However, when defending against an attacke,r your best tactic is to keep obstacles between you and and him. And the best obstacle to keep between you and an attacker is distance. Remember, danger increases with proximity.

The closer an Assassin could get to his target, the more likely that target would not live to see another day. Conversely, the farther away from an attacker you stay, the better off you are. When unable to keep distance between yourself and an attacker, employ blockers and obstacles to stymie his advance. Equally important, fill your hand with *any* weapon you can find, if only a handful of dirt.

Blockers and Obstacles

These consist of anything and everything you can place in your attacker's path to impede his advance, or anything you can use to protect yourself from harm.

Blockers

Anything you can use to ward off an attack or use to counterattack is a blocker. A large book or notebook, for example, can be used as a shield to block punches, kicks, and weapon thrusts.

Shifting to the outside of the attacking arm, the defender uses the large hardback book he is holding to deflect the attacking arm (Illustration 35Ai) or to counterattack into the assailant's elbow.

Having deflected the attacking arm in toward the attacker's centerline (closing off his centerline), the defender counterattacks into the attacker's face with the sharp edge of the book (Illustration 35Bii).

Other examples of blockers include slipping your shoe over your leading/defending hand or wrapping your jacket around your forearm to guard against knife cuts or using a chair like a lion tamer to hold a street beast at bay.

Approached by an attacker while seated in a chair (Illustration 36i), keep your hands up in front (for initial blocking) while placing your feet flat on the floor and shifting your weight slightly forward.

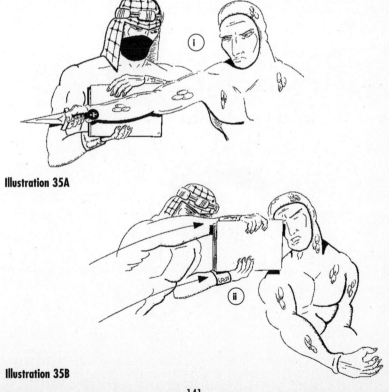

Illustration 35A

Illustration 35B

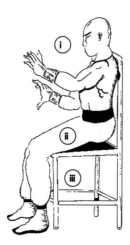

Illustration 36

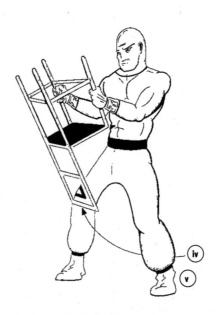

Illustration 37

Quickly slide your legs out to the side and squat (Illustration 36ii), taking your weight off the chair.

As you squat (Illustration 36iii), simultaneously topple the chair over with your butt.

Still squatting, reach down to grip the legs of the toppled chair (Illustration 37iv), pulling it between your legs up to a guard position in front of your chest.

This blocker chair (Illustration 37v) can also be used as a bludgeon to strike or stab (with the legs of the chair) into an attacker.

Obstacles

Obstacles consist of any object (a wall, stairs, sharp corners, etc.) you can shove an attacker into. Correctly using obstacles includes taking advantage of poor positioning on your opponent's part as well as maneuvering an opponent into position.

Street punks know to take advantage of a potential victim leaning into a public phone or leaning over a water fountain, ramming the victim's head into those objects, stunning him. Other tried-and-true obstacle ploys include seizing an attacker's extended arm and levering it against a fixed object such as a counter or a telephone pole in order to break the elbow.

As an assailant thrusts across the horizontal obstacle (store counter; wall; fence; etc.), the defender seizes and jerks the assailant's arm forward (Illustration 38i), turning the arm, disarming the attacker, and breaking the his elbow over the obstacle.

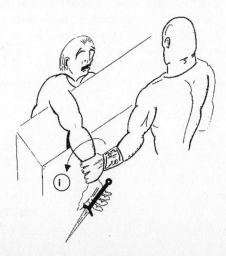

Illustration 38

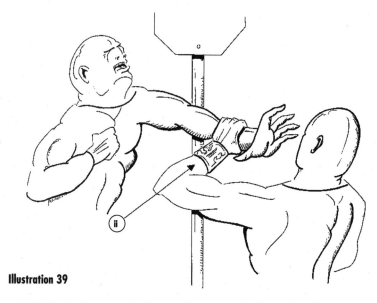

Illustration 39

Taking advantage of a nearby vertical obstacle (telephone pole, fence post, stop sign), the defender seizes the thrusting arm and levers it against the pole (Illustration 39ii), disarming the attacker and breaking the elbow.

Knife Substitutes

Any sharp, pointed object can be used (with various degrees of effectiveness) to stab into vulnerable, soft body targets (eyes, throat, groin). Any edged cutting tool (razor blade, linoleum cutters, etc.) can be used to slash body targets, specifically the throat.

Any pencil, pen, or sharp stick can be held between the fingers (Illustration 40i), seated in the palm and be used as a stabbing weapon.

Note: In the Orient, whole styles of martial arts have been built around the use of simple wooden chopsticks. Any shard of glass (Illustration 40ii), concrete, or metal can effectively double as a stabbing weapon. The serrated edge of a tin can lid (Illustration 40iii) can slash through flesh as easily as a razor blade. Three nails and a *TV Guide*-sized magazine can easily be turned into an effective push dagger (Illustration 40iv). Note: To construct this knife substitute, drive the nails through the open magazine, then roll the

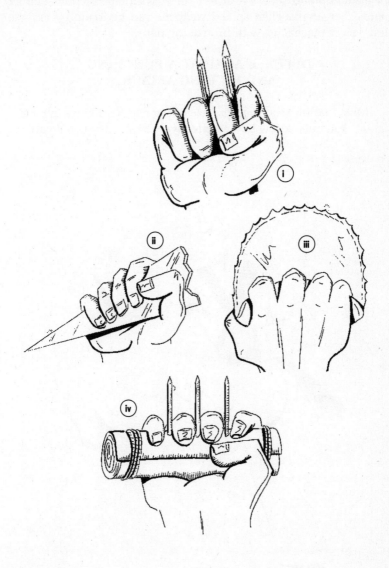

Illustration 40

magazine up and secure it at both ends with tape or thick rubber bands. Larger macelike spiked weapons can be made by embedding larger magazines with protruding nails.

DEFENSE AGAINST A PUNCHING
AND KICKING ATTACK

Most martial arts teach the use of punches and kicks in combination. You must know how to effectively deal with such an attack.

Illustration 41

Targeting The Puncher-Kicker

The fist of an attacker (Illustration 41i) can be counterattacked with bludgeon blows or with stabs when armed with a knife or knife substitute. Splayed hands ("kung-fu claws") can be counterattacked with counterpunches and with grabbing wrenches (designed to break individual fingers).

The wrist (Illustration 41ii) is the weak link between the weapons of the arm (forearm, elbow) and the deadly hand. Wrists can be dislocated and broken using a variety of locks and twists.

The elbow (Illustration 41iii) can be targeted with punches and forceful open-palm blows. The elbow can also be locked out and broken during close-in grappling.

The rear hand (Illustration 41iv) of an attacker must be watched, since his lead hand may be used as a feint to set you up for the real attack from the rear hand. Note: Some martial arts "animal" styles adopt exaggerated stances that draw their rear hands so far back that the hands cease to be an immediate factor in a self-defense situation.

The kicking foot (Illustration 41v) can be countered with forceful "hammer" blows, bludgeon blows, and with stabbing counterattacks from blades and blade substitutes.

When countering a kick unarmed, scoop and seize the attacking leg and run with it, pulling the kicker off balance. During close-in grappling, stomp onto an opponent's foot to distract him and damage the foot, thus impeding his mobility.

The knee of a kicker (Illustration 41vi) can be countered with forceful bludgeon blows and with stabs from knives and knife substitutes. The knee can also be locked out or broken in the same manner as locking out an elbow.

The groin (Illustration 41vii) can be counterattacked each time an attacker raises his leg to kick. Note: Janna fighters seldom kick above the waist in order to prevent exposing their groin and supporting leg to counterattack.

The support leg of a kicker (Illustration 41viii) can be attacked, especially after the kicker has thrown a high kick. Attack an opponent's support leg with sweeping-in kicks and stomps.

The face of an attacker (Illustration 41ix) can be butted during close-in grappling. Note: Any motion (hand feint, object thrown) toward an opponent's face elicits an instinctive flinch reaction that can work to your advantage.

Illustration 42

DEFENSE AGAINST A KICKER

An assailant may decide to attack you only with kicks. Here's how to defeat him.

Countering the Kicker

As the attacker executes his kick (whether a side kick or a forward kick; Illustration 42i), immediately side-shift to the outside of the kicking leg.

As you shift to the outside, bring your hand in under the kicking leg and attack into the attacker's groin (Illustration 42ii) with either a forceful palm blow or a stabbing thrust with a knife or knife substitute.

As one hand attacks the opponent's groin, use your other to jam any potential counterstrike (Illustration 43iii) from your opponent's lead hand.

After striking the groin, use your striking hand to scoop the kicking leg and dump the kicker. If necessary, sweep or stomp the attacker's supporting leg out from under him (Illustration 42iv).

DEFENSE AGAINST A GRAPPLING ATTACK

The same basic hand movements are used when you are defending yourself unarmed as when you are armed. For example, the hammer-fist you administer to an attacking grappler's exposed back is the same motion you use when plunging a knife down into his back.

In order to assure maximum pentration for knife striking, practice as if each knife strike is actually an unarmed strike. This attitude will add extra stunning force to your initial knife strike in case follow-up strikes are required.

DEFENSE AGAINST A "BUM'S RUSH"

As a grappler rushes in (Illustration 43i) head down, his intent is to encircle either your waist or your leading leg. Avoid this by stepping backward.

Immediately counter by striking down onto the attacker's

Illustration 43

exposed spine (Illustration 43ii) or base of the skull with punishing hammer-hand blows or with a blade.

Strike up into the grappler's lowered face with rising knee strikes (Illustration 43iii), uppercut reverse hammer-hand blows, or with a stabbing weapon.

Having closed with a grappler, slide back (Illustration 43iv), pulling the grappler off balance while simultaneously pressing him toward the ground.

DEFENSE AGAINST A FRONT BEAR HUG

As the grappler rushes in (Illustration 44i) intending to encircle your body, step back.

Use the momentum of the attacker to impale his groin (Illustration 44ii) on your rising knee.

In lieu of a rising knee strike, strike up into the attacker's groin (Illustration 44iii) with reverse hammer-hand blows (using the thumb side of the hammer-hand).

Seizing your blade or blade substitute (concealed in the small of your back, belt, etc.; Illustration 44iv) stab up into the attacker's groin or lower abdomen.

Another option is as the grappler closes with you, grab a handful of his hair (Illustration 45v) and force his head back to expose his throat (Illustration 45vi). (For short-haired attackers, press your hand under his nose to force his head back.)

Having used your grip on your attacker's hair to pull his head back and expose his throat, use your knife (Illustration 45vii) or stabbing substitute to strike into your attacker's face, throat (Illustration 45vi), or upper chest. Note: In lieu of a knife or other stabbing weapon, employ hammer-hand blows to crush your attacker's larynx.

As you pull your attacker's head back, sweep his leg out from under him (Illustration 45viii) by kicking back with your own leg.

DEFENSE AGAINST A REAR STRANGLE HOLD

Prevent your attacker from fully encircling your throat by wedging your hand (Illustration 46i) in between your throat and the attacker's arms. At all costs, prevent the attacker's hands from locking together. When possible, bite into the encircling arm to loosen it.

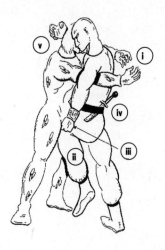

Illustration 44

Illustration 45

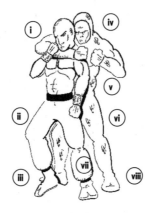

Illustration 46

Illustration 47

As soon as you realize your attacker is attempting to put a strangle hold on you, squat (Illustration 46ii) and shift away from his centerline and escape before the hold can be completed. If the hold has already been completed, dig your chin into the encircling arm and drop your weight to make it more difficult for your attacker to control you (since he must bear all your weight).

To otherwise loosen his grip, stomp on the attacker's foot (Illustration 46iii); head-butt back into his face (Illustration 46iv); strike into his sides, abdomen, and solar plexus with backward elbow strikes (Illustration 46v); and strike back into his groin with hammer-hand blows and wrenching grabs (Illustration 46vi).

Having loosened the attacker's choke hold, coordinate kicking back whichever of your feet is closest to the attacker's centerline (Illustration 46vii) while twisting forward and away from his centerline. As you twist, thrust your hip back simultaneously and dump your attacker to the ground.

A variation: position your foot behind the attacker's outside foot (Illustration 46viii) and kick forward, dumping him backward onto the ground.

DEFENSE AGAINST A HEADLOCK

If your head is encircled by an attacker (Illustration 47i), drop your weight by squatting slightly.

If you are armed with a knife (concealed in your belt or the small of your back), retrieve the blade with your free rear hand (Illustration 47ii) and stab into the attacker's lower back (targeting the spine and kidneys). If you are unarmed, circle your rear hand (Illustration 47ii) up behind the attacker's back to grasp a handful of his hair and pull his head back. (Against a short-haired attacker, lever force against his face—under the nose—and push his head back.)

If you are armed with a knife (concealed in your sock or boot), stab up into the groin, bladder, and lower abdomen of the attacker. If you are unarmed, strike into the attacker's groin (Illustration 47iii) with punishing left hand blows and wrenching grabs. From this position, you can also attack the groin from behind.

Sweeping your left hand down and back, sweep the attacker's leg (Illustration 47iv) out from under him, toppling him forward.

A variation: coordinate sweeping your left hand up behind

153

your attacker's knee (Illustration 47v) at the same time you lever his head back (Illustration 47ii). These combined actions will topple your attacker backward.

DEFENSE AGAINST KNIFE ATTACKS

Not knowing how to defend against a knife attack will get you dead in record time. Knowing the basics is the best beginning.

The Basics of Knife Defense

The same janna blocks used to block unarmed attacks can be used to block knife attacks. Don't let the fact that an attacker is armed with a knife intimidate you: if an attacker can't hit you with a punch, he probably can't hit you with a knife. If you have practiced your unarmed blocking techniques, you have nothing to fear from a knife attacker. All too often, it is the fear of the knife rather than the knife itself that kills people.

Three unbreakable rules must be observed when you find yourself confronted by a knife attacker:

Rule One

Keep as much distance as possible between you and your assailant.

Rule Two

Always get behind an obstacle or pick up a blocker when confronted with a knife.

Rule Three

Always fill your hand with a weapon—any weapon—when confronting a knife. Untrained knife wielders make exaggerated swings that either close off or overly expose their centerlines. These wild swings restrict their follow-up actions.

The Untrained

Untrained attackers slashing along a horizontal plane (Illustration 48i) swing wide outward, exposing their centerline to counterattack, and swing too far inwards, closing off their centerline and making it easy to immobilize their attacking arm by pinning it against their body as they swing inward.

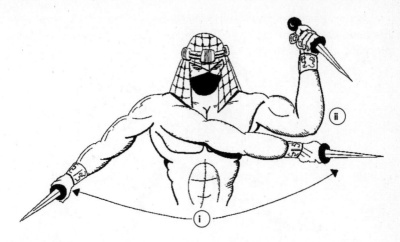

Illustration 48

Attackers drawing weapons high and back (Illustration 48ii) in an exaggerated arc can easily be jammed at the elbow and forearm.

Defense Against the Forward Stab: Technique #1

As the attacker commits to a mid-level knife thrust, shift to the outside of his thrusting arm (Illustration 49i).

As you shift to the outside, counterattack into the elbow (Illustration 49ii) of his thrusting arm with a forceful palm blow/block.

Coordinate counterattacking into the attacker's elbow by bringing your forward hand up and around (Illustration 49iii) the inside of the thrusting arm.

Pulling on the attacker's thrusting arm (forearm or wrist) while pushing the attacking arm's elbow (Illustration 50iv), force the attacker to the ground. Note: This technique also works when pressure is applied at the attacker's shoulder.

If the attacker resists the takedown, sweep his lead foot (Illustration 50v) out from under him by kicking backwards with your foot closest to the attacker. Attention: Never try to hold an attacker, no matter how good of an arm-bar elbow lock or wrist lock you have on him. When applying an arm hold or lock to a violent attacker, break his arm.

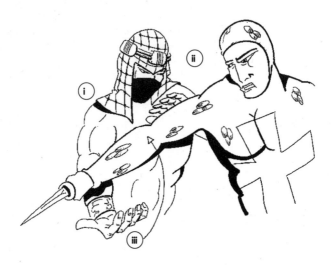

Illustration 49

Illustration 50

Technique #2

As a knife-wielding attacker grips your arm, intent on pulling you into his poised blade, immediately lower your weight back and down (straightening the attacker's gripping arm; Illustration 51i).

Coordinate pulling your weight back and down while rotating your wrist toward the gripping hand's thumb (Illustration 51ii) and apply a countergrip on the attacker's gripping arm.

As the attacker thrusts, shift to the outside (diagonally forward; Illustration 52iii) of the attacker's thrusting arm, all the while retaining your grip on the attacker's other arm.

Coordinate your shifting diagonally forward with drawing the attacker's gripping/gripped arm under his thrusting arm (Illustration 52iv).

Having closed off the attacker's centerline by crossing his arms, counterattack to the back of the attacker's head (Illustration 52v) with an elbow strike. Note: Levering pressure against the back

Illustration 51

Illustration 52

of the attacker's neck (while retaining your grip on his arms) will force him to the ground.

For resisting attackers, kick the attacker's leading leg out from under him (Illustration 52vi), dumping him to the ground.

Defense Against a Rising Knife Attack

Having deflected/blocked the attacker's vertical rising knife strike (Illustration 53i) using a rising half-moon block or an X block, seize a firm grip on his attacking arm and lever it, first in towards his centerline and then suddenly out and up, away from his centerline.

Coordinate raising the attacker's arm up and out with your ducking under the attacker's trapped arm (Illustration 53ii).

Simultaneously with ducking under attacker's trapped arm, pivot to the outside of the attacker's leading foot (Illustration 53iii).

Having pivoted under the attacker's trapped arm and having positioned yourself on the outside of the attacker while retaining

Illustration 53

Illustration 54

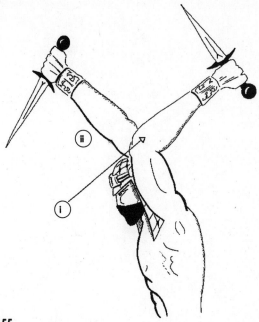

Illustration 55

your grip on his arm, bring the gripped arm down sharply on your shoulder (Illustration 54iv), disarming the attacker and breaking his arm at the elbow.

Sweep the attacker's lead leg out from under him by kicking forward or backward (Illustration 54v), dumping him to the ground.

Retaining your grip on his broken arm, finish the downed attacker with stomps to his head and body.

Defense Against an Overhead Knife Attack

As the attacker draws his knife up and back (in preparation for a downward vertical stab; Illustration 55i), jam his arm at his upturned elbow, forcing his elbow farther up and back and opening him to counterattack. Note: As the attacker's elbow is forced farther up and back, attack his legs with sweeps to topple him backward.

If you are unable to jam the overhead attack before the attacker initiates his downward stroke, strike up into the elbow (Illustration 55ii) with a rising forearm block. Note: Remember

Illustration 56

Illustration 57

that every block is also a strike. Perform every block with the intent to do as much damage to the attacking limb as possible.

Block an overhead stabbing attack using a forearm X block (Illustration 56iii). Once contact has been made, deflect or trap the attacker's arm by turning your block to the side.

Block an overhand stabbing attack by using a rising half-moon block (Illustration 57iv) designed to sweep the attacking hand aside and in toward the attacker's centerline.

Having blocked a downward stab, use your blocking hand to seize a grip on the attacking arm's wrist (Illustration 57v) while simultaneously chopping into the crook of the attacking arm, depleting the strength of the arm. Having greatly weakened the arm and retaining your grip on the attacking arm's wrist, with your other hand in the crook of the attacking arm's elbow, press in with your elbow to lever the attacking arm back (Illustration 57vi), forcing the attacker to the ground. Note: Augment this technique with a leg sweep.

A variation: As your half-moon block deflects the attacker's arm in toward his centerline, grip the attacking arm's wrist, and using the attacker's momentum, direct the descending arc of the knife into the attacker's abdomen (Illustration 57vii), in effect making him stab himself. Note: This technique is aided by your stepping past the attacker on the outside of his leading leg as his momentum impales him on his own knife.

Defense Against A Knife To The Throat (From The Rear)

As the attacker encircles your neck, intent on pressing the knife to your throat or slicing your throat (Ilustration 58i), duck down and shift to the outside (toward the elbow of the encircling arm).

As you shift to the outside, position your inside foot behind your attacker's outside foot (Illustration 58ii).

When necessary, liberally apply softening-up strikes (instep stomps, groin strikes and grabs, and backwards elbow strikes to the solar plexus) to loosen the attacker's grip (Illustration 58iii).

Having ducked out from under the encircling arm, grip the knife-wielding arm (Illustration 59iv) and push it toward the attacker.

Coordinate the pushing of the knife toward your attacker (Illustration 59v) with pulling your other arm (still gripped by the attacker) forward and down. This move turns the attacker into the path of the blade.

Illustration 58

Sweep the attacker's leg out from under him by kicking forward with the leg you previously positioned behind his leg (Illustration 59vi).

DEFENSE AGAINST BLUDGEONS
AND FLEXIBLE WEAPONS

When defending against bludgeons and spinning flexible weapons (chains, nunchakus, etc.), the same rules and tactics apply as when dealing with a knife: keep distance between you and your attacker. Find a shield and weapon(s) to help in your defense.

As with untrained knife wielders, untrained bludgeon wielders use exaggerated inward swings that close off their centerlines (tying up the bludgeon wielder's arms) or wide, outward swings that open their centerline to counterattack.

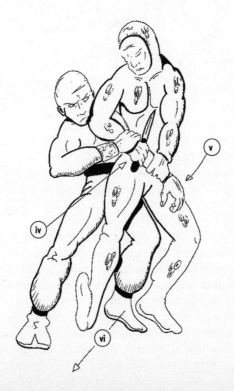

Illustration 59

165

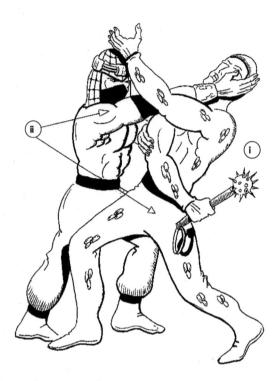

Illustration 60

Bludgeon Defense

Allow the attacker to swing his bludgeon along its exaggerated arc (Illustration 60i) outward or inward. When he swings outward, wait till the bludgeon reaches its farthest outward point, then close and counterattack into his exposed centerline. When the attacker swings his bludgeon inward, close and pin his bludgeon arm after the bludgeon has swung in across his centerline.

Having jammed the bludgeon from returning outward, counterattack into his exposed groin (Illustration 60ii) or face.

When an attacker thrusts his weapon (or fist) forward, duck under the thrusting arm and come up on the outside of the attacking thrusting arm (Illustration 61iii).

Coordinate ducking to the outside of the attacking arm with counterattacking into your attacker's throat or face (Illustration 61iv).

After striking the attacker's face or throat, your inside hand proceeds past the attacker's head and links up with your outside hand behind the attacker's head (Illustration 62v) to complete a half strangle hold that traps the attacker's weapons hand.

Coordinate linking your hands behind the attacker's head and kicking back with your leg closest to the attacker (Illustration 62vi), sweeping him to the ground.

Flexible Weapon Defenses

Flexible weapons are any weapon that can be spun, whipped around, or snapped forward (like a wet towel). Traditional occidental flexible weapons include the medieval chained mace and the combat flail. Flexible weapons in the orient include the nunchakus ("numb-chucks") and the *manrikigusari* (fighting chain). Makeshift flexible weapons include such things as a can of beer tied into a sock, a motorcycle chain, or a heavy electrical cord.

The rules for defending against flexible weapons are the same

Illustration 61

Illustration 62

for all weapons: keep your distance and find a shield and a weapon to turn the odds in your favor. The key to defending against flexible weapons is to interrupt their swings, either by putting an object in the path of their swing or by waiting until the flexible weapon has reached its furthest point outward or inward.

Whatever the particular flexible weapon, flexible weapons are either snapped forward like a wet "rat-tail" towel or swung in one of three ways: over the head, at the side, or in a figure 8.

Many untrained flexible weapons users swing their weapons over their heads (Illustration 63i) in order to intimidate their victims. As flexible weapons technique goes, swinging a flexible weapon over your head is least effective as it exposes you to counterattack.

Flexible weapons spun at the side (Illustration 63ii) usually strike during the downward stroke. A notable exception is nunchakus.

The most efficient way to use a flexible weapon is to spin it in a figure-8 (Illustration 63iii), which allows it to build up momentum and therefore acquire more striking power, thus permitting the wielder to attack inward toward a victim from both sides.

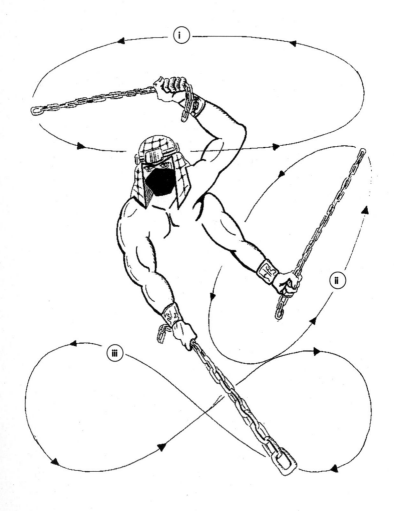

Illustration63

170

CHAPTER TWELVE

The Old Ways

MISCELLANEOUS HISTORICAL ASSASSINATION METHODS

During his life, the prophet Muhammad not only survived numerous pitched battles, but he also survived attempts on his life from bludgeons, strangulation, and even poison. During those times, the conventional dagger to the heart was not an option, so assassins were trained to improvise and find alternative means for disposing of enemies. In the end, it didn't matter what method of murder an assassin used, so long as the job got done.

Death is death no matter what direction it comes from.

Bludgeons

A man once tried to kill Muhammad by hitting him with a huge stone while the prophet was praying. In 750 c.e., 80 ruling Ommayyad Arab princes were invited to a banquet where they were then trapped and clubbed to death by rival Abbasids usurpers staging a coup.

For medieval assassins, the use of bludgeons included any club that could bash a person's brains in, any heavy object that could be dropped on a person, or the dropping of the person himself from a high position. Mastery of the use of bludgeons included pushing an enemy target off a high balcony or in front of an oncoming wagon. (A modern translation of this would be shoving an enemy in front of an oncoming truck, auto, or subway train, onto a sharp object, or into a live electrical device or wire that would electrocute him, all of which are methods commonly used by today's Assassins.) Care would be taken when choosing a bludgeon, avoiding a top-heavy bludgeon that would throw the Assassin off balance.

When striking with a bludgeon, Assassins used a chopping motion, (rather than that extended follow-through technique your Little League coach taught you, as this would open the Assassin to counterattack).

Strangulation

Members of the Quraysh tribe once tried to strangle Muhammad but were prevented from doing so by Abu-Bakr. After the fall of Alamut and the scattering of the Persian branch of the Assassins, many assassins settling in India abandoned the assassin's trademark dagger for the equally effective strangulation art of the Kali cult of Thuggee. Despite the Thuggee raising strangulation to an art form, there remains only two basic types of strangulation: manual strangulation and strangulation by a weapon.

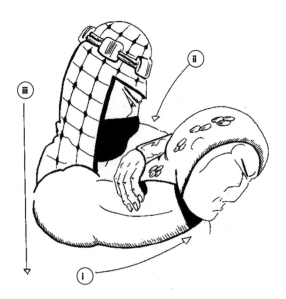

Illustration 64

Illustration 65

Manual and Weapon Strangulation Techniques
Having approached his victim from behind, the Assassin would slide his arm around the victim's throat (Illustration 64i) and strike back forcefully into the victim's larynx with the "blade" of his forearm.

Seating the victim's throat in the crook of his elbow (Illustration 64ii), he would drop his other arm behind the victim's head, locking his hand onto the bicep of the forward arm.

The Assassin would then complete his strangle lock by dropping his weight down (Illustration 64iii) as he pulled the victim down and back, forcing his head forward.

Note: Performed quickly and forcefully, this "yoke" strangulation technique crushed the victim's larynx or broke his neck.

In lieu of a manual strangulation, any stout stick or similar object (Illustration 65iv) could be used to crush a victim's larynx or strangle the life out of him.

Note: For those interested in an in-depth study of the ancient and modern art of strangulation, as well as a history of the Kali-Thuggee cult of India, read *The Ancient Art of Strangulation* by Dr. Haha Lung (available from Paladin Press).

Poison

The Arab historic use of poison chronicler Al-Jami-us-Sahih relates how a woman once tried to kill Muhammad by poisoning his meat. Poisoning your enemies remains a time-honored Middle Eastern tradition. In fact, Ali, patron of the Shiite branch of Islam from which the Order of Assassins descended, was murdered by a poisoned sword. In the 7th century, what the troops of Utbah (a lieutenant of Caliph Omar) thought was poisoned food set as a trap by their foes turned out to be harmless rice (which the Arabs had never seen before). While somewhat humorous, this story illustrates that poisoning—or at least the fear of poisoning—was common practice in Middle East at the time.

References to poisoning (individual and large scale) as an accepted tactic in warfare are numerous in Middle Eastern history. During the Second Arab War (722-737 C.E.), conquering Arabs poisoned the entire water supply of the city of Bab al Abwab on the Caspian Sea in an effort to bring the fierce Khazar tribes of the Caucasus under control. The Assassin use of poisons ran the gamut from a toxic powder used to blind an enemy during one-on-one combat to sending poisoned gifts to enemy officials.

Assassin sappers always poisoned their blades, and given their mastery of poisons, dying instantly from a straight thrust to the heart was much preferable to the lingering agony a victim could expect from just a scratch from an Assassin blade. When Prince Edward of England (1239-1307) was wounded by an Assassin wielding a poisoned blade, only his wife's quick action of sucking the poison from her husband's wound saved his life. Though in agony for weeks, the prince survived to become King Edward I.

Poisons were useful when more subtlety and subterfuge was called for. Many influential figures in Middle Eastern (and European) politics in the Middle Ages died of "dysentery" or "fevers," often fortuitously on the eve of a great battle or just before signing a pivotal treaty. Given the subtlety of poison use, we will never know how many medieval notables who died of "natural causes" actually succumbed to poison. However, you will recall the fact that in 1277 Mameluke warlord (de facto Assassin grand master) Rukn Baibars got his cups mixed up and accidently poisoned himself while trying to poison a rival, which testifies to the widespread use of poison as a viable political tool at the time.

Assassin grand masters referred to the use of poison as "giving the gift." A targeted individual might receive—via a third party—a gift of a unique perfume. Harmless in and of itself, when the innocuous fragrance was mixed with another equally innocent perfume, the two created deadly fumes. Note: Unique perfumes were often used as recognition signals between undercover Assassin agents and their contacts.

Deadly perfumes were distilled from common weeds and flowers. For example, lilly of the valley, when correctly fermented, produces a deadly nerve toxin. Other Assassin poisons came from such mundane sources as rhubarb leaves, mushrooms, and fruits such as apricots, plums, and almonds. Still other Assassin poisons were extracted from such creatures as snakes and scorpions. In some cases, the creatures themselves—strategically placed— became the weapon. Yet another Assassin gift of poison, believed imported from the Far East, was to send the targeted person ornate garments woven from the silk of worms fed on the beans of the castor plant. (Ricin, considered one of the five most toxic substances in the world, is derived from the beans of the castor plant.)

Over time, the poison in garments woven from these deadly silk threads would first make the person ill and eventually kill them. Rings and other gifts of jewelry were also impregnated with poison hidden under a thin gold or silver veneer, which was designed to wear off or dissolve after the jewelry was warmed by the wearer's skin, releasing the poison beneath.

Medieval royalty, paranoid of poisoning, employed food tasters to sample food and drink before meals to insure that the food and drink was safe. Assassin agents, planted in these rival courts as food tasters, would often have to eat poisoned food and drink poisoned wine in order to allay suspicions of the targeted king or prince. Sometimes these agents would have an antidote, but other times they willingly consumed slow-acting poison, knowing they would die but remaining willing to sacrifice themselves in order to entice the targeted official to eat or drink the substance. Often a targeted official would be fed an initially harmless poison that was activated only after the victim ate a second ingredient. One Assassin extortion ploy called for poisoning an official and then offering to sell him the antidote in return for money or cooperation. Given the terror mere mention of the Assassins evoked, just telling a frightened official he had been poisoned, in lieu of actually poisoning him, was often enough to elicit cooperation or a healthy contribution to the Assassin cause. Kings and courtiers reluctant to assist the Assassin cause were often secretly given enough poison to make them terribly ill, but not enough to kill them. The grand master could then generously send his "personal physician" (in reality another Assassin agent) to "cure" the stricken king. Grateful, the cured king would then aid the Assassin cause. A variation of this ploy helped Assassin agents posing as physicians (who just happened to have the exact cure a stricken official needed) to get posted to a rival official's court.

Assassins made a practice of ingesting small amounts of poison (sometimes over a period of years) to build up their immunity to the poisons, especially those they used regularly. Evidently, it was considered bad form to die from accidentally scratching yourself with your own poisoned blade!

This slow process of creating immunity against poison by administering small quantities of a toxin or virus until sufficient antibodies have been built up is known as mithridatizing, a word deriving from an ancient king of Asia Minor, Mithridates VI (120-63 B.C.E.). Paranoid about assassination, over the years Mithridates ingested regular small doses of poison in order to build up his immunity. Ironically, after his final defeat at Nicopolis, Mithridates tried to kill himself with poison but failed because of the immunity he had built up over the years. He finally had to order one of his mercenaries to kill him with a sword.

The Assassins' masterful use of poisons inevitably led to tales that the cult possessed the secret of killing with just a touch, a look, or the curse of a magic spell. Such fantastic tales, encouraged by the grand master's propaganda machine, are similar to tales of the infamous dim-mak ("death touch") of ancient China. (Note: Paladin Press has the most extensive library of dim-mak manuals available, all written by acclaimed—and very dangerous—instructor Erle Montaigue.)

Many in the Orient believed ninja possessed the power to strike an enemy in a way that would interrupt the natural flow of his *ki* (vital energy), causing the victim to drop dead at a later time, a time chosen by the ninja. Science dismisses such mysticism but does concede that an accomplished martial artist—one knowledgable in anatomy—could strike a victim and create a blood clot that in turn could cause a heart attack or stroke at a later time. Such blows could also rupture internal organs, causing the victim to bleed to death internally. Other ninja methods were actually "one-eyed snake" ploys, which were killing methods (such as poisons) designed to mimic killing techniques in the same vein as dim-mak.

Eastern religious proscriptions against autopsies prevented the discovery of foul play by poison (or other internal methods), as they did in Europe.

The Crusades and their aftermath opened Europe to many Middle Eastern ideas and goods. Coffee (from the Arabic word *qahwa*) was introduced into Europe by returning Crusaders, as were other formerly unknown Middle Eastern foods and spices. Heretofore unknown medicines and knowledge of human anatomy were also introduced into Europe by the Crusades.

In Europe, as in the Orient, religious restrictions against human dissection meant there was no way to detect the presence of poisons in a dead body until the Vatican authorized autopsies in the 15th century. Machiavellian individuals and families—the 14th-15th century Medici and Borgias, for example—are infamous for taking advantage of this murderous loophole.

As in the Middle East, there is no way of telling how many royals and notables of medieval Europe, listed as having died of natural causes, actually drank from the Assassin's bitter cup. Indeed, while we will never know the extent of the practice of poison craft in medieval Europe, we do know that paranoia over poisoning was widespread as Europe entered the Renaissance, as evidenced by the fact that poison plays a pivotal role in Shakespeare's *Romeo and Juliet* (1594) and again in *Hamlet* (1600).

The Modern Poison Threat

There is a widespread fear that, sooner or later, some fanatical terrorist group will get their hands on a nuclear weapon. The break up of the Soviet Union has made this grim scenario even more likely, but while attention has been focused on moves intended to restrict the spread of materials and technology needed to build nuclear weapons, trans-Islamic terrorists and their supporter states are concentrating their efforts in other directions.

Author and Middle East expert Laurie Mylroie, who investigated the World Trade Center bombing, warns that Iraqi sleeper agents connected with Abdel-Rahman's Jihad organization are still operating in the United States. What is most alarming is that one of these agents is reportedly an Iraqi scientist living in New York City, active in the field of genetic engineering. What if such a scientist—one with trans-Islamic sympathies or one whose family was being held hostage by a terrorist state—decided to help trans-Islamic terrorists acquire not a nuclear bomb, but equally deadly chemical or biological weapons? What if a fanatical religious fundamentalist group decided to use a chemical or biological weapon in an indiscriminate attack on civilians similar to the World Trade Center bombing?

It has already happened. On March 20, 1995, the fanatical Japanese religious cult Aum Shinri Kyo unleashed a deadly sarin nerve gas attack on a crowded Tokyo subway, killing 12 and injuring thousands. The cult had manufactured the gas themselves.

In a related and grossly underreported incident, two members of the cult were arrested entering the United States, carrying blueprints and formulas for the manufacture of sarin. Their travel plans included a stop at Disneyland.

During the Iran-Iraq War, Saddam Hussein used nerve gas against rebel Muslim Kurds and against rival Muslim Iranians. If a Muslim leader like Saddam Hussein thinks nothing of unleashing nerve gas on his brother Muslims, how can we expect him to treat infidels in the West who oppose him?

In March of 1996 the CIA revealed that Libya was (and still is) busy building "the world's largest underground chemical-weapons plant" designed to manufacture mustard gas and nerve agents. According to experts, "Unless destroyed. . .the new factory could keep Qaddafi's favorite terrorists well stocked with chemical poisons for decades." Given Qaddafi's track record and his dedication to trans-Islamicism, is there any doubt that, sooner or later, a small canister of one of these deadly chemicals will find its way onto a commercial jetliner departing North Africa, bound for Europe or the United States?

What about poisoning an enemy with a biological weapon? How hard would it be for a Middle Eastern terrorist group to unleash a modern-day plague on the West?

Consider this troubling news bit: On May 11, 1995, authorities raided the home of a self-styled microbiologist in Lancaster, Ohio, where it was discovered that the man was holding bubonic plague (*Yersinia pestis*) bacteria that he purchased through the mail from a Maryland laboratory supplier.

Or consider this: The African ebola virus has a 77 percent fatality rate. What if a Middle Eastern terrorist purposely infected himself with the virus (or a similar deadly virus) 24 hours prior to boarding a plane for La Guardia or JFK? How long would it take just one infected terrorist riding a New York subway to infect thousands, and each of those thousands to, in turn, infect a thousand others? And let's not forget the hundreds of travelers the terrorist deliberately brushes up against, sneezes on, and kindly helps with their bags while passing through the airport terminal, hundreds boarding scores of planes bound for dozens of other major cities in the United States.

A farfetched scenario? Remember that we are talking about the same fanatics who think nothing of strapping bombs to their bodies before boarding buses filled with children. And never forget that we are talking about killers who take pride in tracing themselves back through the most murderous of lineages to the Old Man of the Mountain.

Glossary

Alamutines: Synonym for the Order of Assassins

Allah: Pre-Islamic lunar war god; god of Islam

al-jebr: Calculation; used by the Order of Assassins as a synonym for strategic and tactical planning.

al-najash: Trick; Assassin strategy.

asas: Foundation. Possible source of English word *assassin*.

assassin: Members of the Nizari Isma'ili sect. May be a corruption of *hashishin*, meaning "those who use hashish."

balam: "Grabbing the ox by the horns." An Assassin grappling technique.

batsh: Grasp; Assassin grappling technique.

betyls: Sacred stones.

burnus: Hooded cloak worn by Assassins.

dabb: Lizard; Assassin breaking & entering/stealth technique.

daughters of Allah: Manat, al-Uzza, and al-Lat, also known as the high flying cranes. Pre-Islamic goddesses.

dayes: Missionaries. Highest level of four major operations sections within the Order of Assassins.

Effrengi: A Frank. A generic term used by Muslims for Europeans that was based upon the erroneous belief that all crusaders were French.

fedayeen: Men of sacrifice; Muslim warriors.

fidavis: Devoted ones. Third level of four major operations sections with the Order of Assassins.

Five Noxious Ones, the: Variations of Assassin *janna* (unarmed combat). Taken from the five creatures pilgrims are allowed to slay while on *hajj*: crows, kites, scorpions, rats, and biting dogs.

Franj: Generic name used by Muslims to denote crusaders. Also based upon the erroneous belief that all crusaders were French.

ghazi: A Muslim warrior who has participated in *jihad*.

ghira: A feeling of anger felt when one's honor is challenged. Similar to the Asian concept of "face."

hadith: Records of the sayings and acts of the prophet Muhammed collected after his death.

hajj: Pilgrimage. Specifically, obligatory pilgrimage to the Ka'Ba in Mecca.

halka: "Circle" or lodge; an organized cell of the Order of Assassisns.

hanif: A holy man; pure.

hanifyya: Muslim religious practices believed derived from Abraham.

haram: Forbidden, taboo. In English, *harem*.

harba: A short spear.

harj: Killing.

Hashimite: A Muslim sharing common ancenstry with Muhammed. Possible source of the English word *assassin*, corrupted from *hashishin*.

hashishin: English synonym for Assassins based upon the erroneous belief that Assassins used hashish.

Hubal: Pre-Islamic god of the Quraysh tribe.

Hums: Puritanical Islamic confederation sect fiercely devoted to Mecca.

Iblis: Satan.

ifreet: A leader of Jinn.

imam: A teacher. In Shiite belief, a divinely inspired prophet.

janna: To hide; the Assassin art of stealth and unarmed combat.

jihad: Striving; holy war against evil.

jinn (also djinn): Covered. In English, *genie*. In Arabic-Islamic mythology, jinn are spirits, both good and evil, composed of smokeless flame that have the power to influence thoughts and actions in humans. Similar to the Christian concept of demons.

Ka'Ba (also Kaba and Cabala): The "Cube." Islam's most holy shrine. Located in Mecca, it houses the sacred black stone, holiest of Muslim relics.

kadi (also qadi and qaadee): Judge.

karaamaat: Supernatural or quasi-miraculous feats often performed by Assassin grand masters to increase their prestige.

karr wa farr: Charging and fleeing. Arabic method of warfare characterized by guerrilla-like strikes designed to strike an enemy and then quickly retreat.

kefiyas: Arab face and head wrap.

khilwat: Silence; meditation methods used by Arabic mystics.

Koran (also Qur'an and Quran): Muslim holy book. Allah's revelations to Muhammed collected and codified after the prophet's death.

laziks: First level of four major operations sections within the Order of Assassins.

qisas: Retribution; making a thing equal with another, as in making the punishment fit the crime.

Quraysh: Tribe into which Muhammed was born; dominant tribe in Arabia at the time of Muhammed; traditional guardians of the Ka'Ba.

rafig: Friends; second level of four major operations sections within the Order of Assassins.

rukn: Stone.

Saracen: Generic name used by European crusaders to denote all Muslims. From the Greek *Sarakenos*, originally referring specifically to nomadic Turks on the Syrian border.

Seveners: Name applied to the Ismaili branch of Shiite Islam.

sharif: Honored title given to male descendants of Muhammed.

Shiite: One of the two main branches of Islam; followers of Ali.

shirk: In Islam, the greatest of sins, that of ascribing equals to Allah (such as the "daughters" of Allah).

shvoye: Patience acquired through the practice of *khilwat*.

Silver Band, the: Name by which the Assassins referred to themselves in English; derived from the silver band said to hold the three pieces of the black stone of the Ka'Ba together.

Sufism: Islamic mystical movement originating in the 8th century.

Sunna (also Sunnite): One of two main branches of Islam; followers of the Caliph line established after Muhammed's death.

taqiyah: Shiite practice of denying their faith in times of danger; Assassin art of disguise.

tarahhub: Ascetic practices used by Assassins both for purifying and strengthening the mind and body.

Bibliography

Al-Ashmawy, Sai'd. "Islam's Real Agenda." *Reader's Digest* (January 1996): 156-160.

Baghdadi, Ali. "Who is the Real Terrorist?" *The Final Call* (February 2, 1996): 13, 31.

Baily, Hester. *The Spirit of Masonry*.

Coil, Henry Wilson. *Coil's Masonic Encyclopedia*.

Crompton, Paul. *The Complete Martial Arts*. Roxby Productions, Ltd.

Davis, James D. "Farrakhan's Remarks Ring True For Some." *Ft. Lauderdale Sun-Sentinel* (March 18, 1994).

Dobson, Christopher. *Black September: Its Short, Violent History*. New York: Macmillan, 1973.

Dorressee, Jean. *The Secret Books of the Egyptian Gnostics*. Rochester, VT: Inner Traditions Intl., Ltd., 1986.

Duke, Steven B. and Gross, Albert C. *America's Longest War*. New York: G.P. Putnam's Sons, 1993.

El-Amin, Mustafa. *Freemasonry, Ancient Egypt & the Islamic Destiny*. New Jersey: New Mind Productions, 1988.

Eerdmans' Handbook to the World's Religions. Michigan: William B. Eerdmans Publishing Co., 1982.

Farah, C.E. *Islam, Beliefs and Practices*. 1970.

Frankel, Bruce. "Terrorism Conspiracy Trial Goes to Jury." *USA Today* (September 25, 1995): 1A.

Frankel, Bruce. "Sheik guilty in terror plot." *USA Today* (October 2, 1995: 1A.

Franzius, Enno. *History of the Order of Assassins*. New York: Funk & Wagnalls, 1969.

Ganley, Elaine. "Islamic Militants Recruit in Europe." *Associated Press/Cleveland Plain Dealer* (July 30, 1995): 13A.

Jonas, George. *Vengeance: The True Story of an Israeli Counter-Terrorist Team*. 1985.

Katz, Lee Michael. "Farrakhan's visits abroad denounced." *USA Today* (February 15, 1996): 6A.

Khan, Dr. Muhammad Mushin. *The Translation of the Meaning of Sahih Al-Bukhari*. Pakistan: Kazi Publications, 1979.

Khan, Dr. Muhammad Mushin. *The Translation of the Meanings of Summarized Sahih Al-Bukhari*. Riyadh: Maktaba Dar-us-Salam Publishing, 1994.

Knappert, Jan. *African Mythology*. London: Diamond Books, 1990.

La Barre, Weston. *The Ghost Dance*. Dell Publishing, 1972.

Laqueur, Walter. *Terrorism*. Boston: Little, Brown & Little, 1977.

Latham, Edward. *A Dictionary of Names, Nicknames & Surnames of*

Persons, Places & Things. London: George Routledge & Sons, Ltd., 1904.

Liu, Melinda. "Meet me in Manhattan." *Newsweek* (October 2, 1995): 49.

Lung, Dr. Haha. *The Ancient Art of Strangulation*. Boulder: Paladin Press, 1995.

Lung, Dr. Haha. *Ninja Craft*. Ohio: Alpha Publications. 1996.

Mackey, Albert G. *Mackey's Revised Encyclopedia of Freemasonry*.

McClintock, John and Strong, James. *Encyclopedia of Biblical, Theological, and Ecclesiastical Literature*. Michigan: Baker Book House, 1981 (Reprint Edition).

Morey, Robert. *The Islamic Invasion: Confronting the World's Fastest Growing Religion*. Oregon: Harvest House Publishers, 1992.

Mylrorie, Laurie. "Saddam and Terrorism: The WTC Bombing." *Newsweek* (October 17, 1994): 30.

New American Desk Encyclopedia. New York: Penguin Books, 1989.

Omar, Ralf Dean. *Death on Your Doorstep: 101 Weapons in the Home*. Ohio: Alpha Publications of Ohio, 1993.

Perry, Marvin. *Unfinished Journey: A World History*. Boston: Houghton Mifflin Co., 1980.

Peters, F.E. *The Hajj: The Muslim Pilgrimage to Mecca and the Holy Places*. New Jersey: Princeton University Press, 1994.

Taymeeyah, Ibn (translated by Philips, Abu Ameenah Bilal). *Essay on the Jinn*. Riyadh: International Islamic Publishing House, 1989.

Pickthall, Muhammad (translator). *The Glorious Qur'an*. Libya: Islamic Call Society.

Ravenscroft, Trevor. *The Spear of Destiny*. Maine: Samuel Weiser, Inc., 1982.

Robinson, John J. *Dungeon, Fire & Sword. The Knights Templars in the Crusades*. New York: M. Evans & Co., 1991.

Sadler, Barry. *Casca #13: The Assassin*. New York: Jove Books, 1988.

Skinner, Dirk. *Street Ninja: Ancient Secrets for Today's Mean Streets*. New York: Barricade Books, 1995.

About the Author

Dr. Haha Lung is the author of more than a dozen books dealing with the "darker side" of the martial arts, forbidden killing techniques, and historical and modern secret societies. His previous book from Paladin Press is *The Ancient Art of Strangulation*.